incmes

3 skin

Cleen — Gilana 4B
Cell = 215-280-2556

Nov 15   Th) Deposit
          } Voucher
   SEC   1st
           $475
           essential

Dec 1   fully Refund

Stenton avenue
        3B

Elkins

* Enthusiastic

(Family network intact)

The NEW Word Power

The South African Handbook of Grammar, Style and Usage

David Adey
Margaret Orr
Derek Swemmer

AD DONKER PUBLISHER

Published in 1996 by
AD DONKER PUBLISHERS (PTY) LTD
A DIVISION OF JONATHAN BALL PUBLISHERS (PTY) LTD
P O Box 33977
Jeppestown 2043

Reprinted 1999

ISBN 0 86852 212 0

Design by Michael Barnett, Johannesburg
Typesetting and reproduction by Book Productions, Pretoria
Cover reproduction by RT Sparhams (Pty) Ltd, Johannesburg
Printed and bound by National Book Printers, Drukkery Street, Goodwood,
Western Cape

Preface

The New Word Power follows on the success of the 'old' *Word Power* which has been in print since 1989. It is aimed at all those who need to use English, particularly in an academic or a business environment. This clear, concise and accessible handbook offers guidance on thorny issues of South African English usage, style, grammar and expression. The book offers assistance with the mechanics of grammar and sentence structure, concentrates on vocabulary and the accurate selection of words, and has entries devoted to business and academic writing skills.

The entries in this handbook reflect a wide range of common problems encountered by students and other users of English. The authors have all taught English for a number of years and have also 'manned' Grammarphone – a telephone advice service run by the English Academy. Persistent problems and common queries have found their way into this handbook, accompanied by simple, clear explanations; rules; mnemonics, and useful advice. The approach in *The New Word Power* is not a prescriptive one, although words and forms of expression that are unacceptable in South African usage are clearly explained. An attempt has been made, rather, to provide a blend of traditional and modern examples to reinforce explanation and commentary.

The content of *The New Word Power* has been expanded and revised, and the layout has been updated and made more user-friendly with – in particular – the second language speaker in mind.

ou find what you are looking for in this handbook?

LPHABETICAL ORDER.

a dictionary or telephone directory, the entries are arranged
alphabetical order, and there are clues called 'running
headers', at the top of the page to tell you whereabouts you are in
the alphabet. So, you can use your scanning skills to flip through
the book, looking at the top outside corners of the pages until
you find the letter of the alphabet you need, then slow down until
you find the particular item you want.

• USE THE INDEX.
At the very end of this handbook you will find an index. This
index (also arranged alphabetically) will give you a list of all the
items dealt with in this handbook, with the relevant page
numbers for each entry.

Sometimes you may be looking for general information –
about business writing, or verbs, for example. Under general
headings, the index will refer you to places where you might find
information about your general topic. It will also list topics that
are related to your general topic.

• USE GENERAL CATEGORIES.
Say you are looking for an explanation of 'enjambement'. But
you don't know that it is called 'enjambement'. In fact you want
to find out the technical term, as well as the explanation! So
where do you start? Start with what you know, and start with the
most general category. You know it's some kind of poetic device.
So, use the index and try looking up 'poetry', 'poetic devices', or
– getting even more general – 'literary devices'. Flip back
through the book and glance quickly at the entries mentioned in
the index. You'll find it soon! (PS: It is on pages 325 – 340).

• START SOMEWHERE.
If you're not sure what you're actually looking for, start by
reading a general entry on the topic, or on a related topic. There
are numerous cross references in most of the entries, so you're
bound to find a signpost to the sub-topic or the particular aspect
of the topic that you're looking for.
Happy travelling!

A, a

1. The indefinite article, **a**, is used before words beginning with a consonant, except for the silent or unsounded 'h'.

a rondavel	a koppie	a dictionary
a history	a humanitarian	a human being
BUT an historical event		

2. **A** is also used before words beginning with 'u', when that 'u' is sounded like a 'y'.

a uniform	a university	a united South Africa
BUT an undercover agent		an underdone steak

See: **An; Articles**

Abbreviations

1. An abbreviation is a shortened form of a word and is formed by omitting some of its letters. The purpose is to save the writer's time, but abbreviations are used to a greater or lesser degree depending on the type of writing composed. They are used frequently in technical writing, timetables, advertisements, telegrams, e-mail, telexes and reference books.
   (A contraction is a shortened form of a word or phrase, in which the missing letters may be indicated by an apostrophe (can't, he'd, you'll, should've)).

See: **Contractions**

2. In most printed matter a full-stop is used after abbreviations.
   However, when an abbreviation ends on the same letter which
   completes the original word, no full-stop is necessary.

> Mr, Revd, Miss, Mrs, Ms, Ltd and Dr do not have
> any full-stops.
>
> BUT   Prof. does have a full-stop.

3. Abbreviations with several capitals and acronyms made up of
   initial capitals do not take full-stops.

SABC	ISCOR	Unesco	Unisa
COSATU	NUMSA	NEHAWU	RDP

See: **Acronyms**

4. Initials of personal names require full-stops.

A.D. Adey	M. H. Orr	D.K. Swemmer

5. It is becoming the modern practice to omit full-stops
   altogether. (This practice has largely been followed by the
   authors.)

6. The plurals of most abbreviations are formed by simply
   adding an 's'. Some plurals are formed by repeating the letter.
   Units of measure are abbreviated identically in the singular
   and plural.

	MPs	BAs	the 1990s
BUT	pp (pages)	ll (lines)	
AND	one cm	thirty cm	357 km

See: **Numbers**

7. AD (*Anno Domini*) and BC (Before Christ) are written with

capitals, but pm (*post meridiem*) and am (*ante meridiem*) are not.

8. In formal writing (such as academic essays, or business letters) it is generally regarded as unacceptable to use the ampersand (&) or plus sign (+) instead of the word 'and'.

9. When an abbreviation which takes a full-stop occurs at the end of a sentence, it is incorrect to add an extra full-stop. However, a comma will follow when such an abbreviation occurs at the end of a phrase or clause in a sentence which continues.

> Themba cleared his throat awkwardly and mumbled 'Sorry, Prof.'
> 'I'm sorry Prof.,' he repeated, 'I didn't mean to miss the exam.'

10. Use abbreviations only when you are sure that your reader will understand them. Remember that they will slow up your readers while they convert the shortened form into its original version.

-able, -ible

1. Both **-ible** and **-able** are root affixes that refer to ability.

> expressible   able to be expressed
> practicable   able to be put into practice

2. With one or two exceptions, **-ible** is used in words derived from Latin, while **-able** is found in words taken from French (ami-able) or Anglo-Saxon (work-able). A good dictionary will supply you with these derivations.

Abstract nouns

1. An abstract noun refers to something intangible or that which cannot be discerned by the five senses. Abstract nouns name –

- qualities: width, height, depth
- concepts: beauty, truth, flight
- actions: arrival, departure
- emotions: love, hate, hunger

2. Abstract nouns can be formed from nouns, adjectives and verbs by adding suffixes, thereby coming to mean a state or quality which is not concrete.

Formed from nouns:		
	boredom	childhood
	chauvinism	scholarship
	democracy	
Formed from adjectives:		
	freedom	communism
	morality	sharpness
Formed from verbs:		
	temptation	precedence
	speculation	agreement

See: **Nouns; Suffixes**

3. When you use an abstract noun to refer to the general concept or emotion, it does not take an article. You only use an article with an abstract noun when you are referring to a specific aspect of the general concept or emotion.

> Freedom of speech is enshrined in the Constitution.
>
> BUT
>
> Flexitime offers me the freedom to plan my working day to suit myself.
>
> Love makes the world go round.
>
> All we need is love.
>
> BUT
>
> The love I feel for my children is surprisingly strong.
>
> Patriotism is the love of one's country.

See: **Articles**

Abstractions   Norman Lear
Bruce – New York

1. Abstractions are ideas or visionary concepts expressed in general or abstract terms. Abstractions need not only be lofty philosophical terms. Any term, removed of its concrete, specific attributes, can become an abstraction.

> For example, one can talk about marriage in the abstract –
> not your marriage or mine, or Charles and Diana's – but marriage
> as a general concept: 'Marriage' then becomes an abstraction.

2. Abstractions are often used to excess by people such as politicians, in order to hide ugly realities.

Abstraction	Concrete Meaning
Unrest	Riots and chaos
Resettlement	Forced eviction and removal of entire communities
Pacification	Bombing people

See: **Euphemisms; Wordiness**

3. Abstractions are, by their very nature, vague terms. If you use them, you need to make their meaning more precise by offering your reader concrete examples of what you mean.

Accents

1. Accent refers to the stress placed on the syllables of a word. Each word has a primary or main stress on one of its syllables. Other syllables receive secondary or tertiary stress.

2. The stressed syllable in a word is indicated, in most dictionaries, by a raised point ·, or mark `, placed after the syllable which receives primary stress.

3. Stress patterns in English often depend on the part of speech.

11

Nouns:	con·vict (*con* is stressed)
	per·mit (*per* is stressed)
Verbs:	convict· (*vict* is stressed)
	permit· (*mit* is stressed)

4. Accent can also mean a style of pronunciation, as in 'she has a strong Afrikaans accent.' The current trend is to downplay the importance of pronunciation and accent in the acquiring of English as a second language. Adult second language learners almost never lose their first language accent. Provided that it is not so deviant as to obscure meaning, a non-native accent should not be stigmatized or regarded as wrong.

See: **Pronunciation; Standard English**

Accept, except

1. **Accept** is a verb which means to consent to something, or to regard with favour.

> I accepted his proposal of marriage.
> We accept the Bill of Rights as a fundamental document.

2. **Except** is a preposition meaning 'not including'

> Everyone, except those with prior commitments, is required to attend the meeting.

3. As a verb, 'to **except**' means 'to exclude'.

> 'All men are chauvinists - present company excepted, of course!'

See: **Except; Homonyms**

Accommodation

1. This abstract noun is the general term referring to furnished or
   unfurnished rooms in a flat, house, hotel, or hostel. It does not
   take an article.

> I am looking for accommodation in Cape Town.
> Accommodation can be a major problem when one moves to a
> new city.
> I would like to book accommodation for the second week of July.

See: **Abstract nouns; Articles**

2. Note the spelling: two Cs, two Ms and one T.

Acronym

1. An acronym is a word usually formed from the initial letters
   of a name, especially where several words make up the name.
   As the word gains more and more acceptance the practice is to
   move from writing it all in capital letters (upper case) to using
   a capital letter only for the first letter – as in *Unisa* for
   *Univ*ersity of *S*outh *A*frica.

> *Cosatu* from *C*ongress *o*f *S*outh *A*frican *T*rade *U*nions;
> *MOTH* from *M*emorable *O*rder of *T*in *H*ats;
> *NASA* from *N*ational *A*eronautics and *S*pace *A*dministration;
> *SADTU* from *S*outh *A*frican *D*emocratic *T*eachers *U*nion;
> *Unesco* from *U*nited *N*ations *E*ducational, *S*cientific and
> *C*ultural *O*rganization

2. Some acronyms are words derived from the initial letters of
   other words, often when these words describe the
   phenomenon defined by the acronym. As such words
   gradually gain acceptance as nouns, their origins as acronyms
   may become obscure to most users of English.

13

> **Aids** from **a**cquired **i**mmune **d**eficiency **s**yndrome;
> **Awol** from **a**bsent **with**out **l**eave;
> **laser** from **l**ight **a**mplification by **s**timulated **e**mission of **r**adiation;
> **radar** from **r**adio **d**etection **a**nd **r**anging.

See: **Abbreviations**

Active, passive

1. A verb is in the **active** voice if the subject of the sentence is the person or thing that performs the action described by the verb.

> Six thousand students **wrote** the Practical English examination.

2. A verb is in the **passive** voice when the subject of the sentence is NOT the 'doer' or performer of the action described by the verb.

> The Practical English examination **was written** by six thousand students.

3. The **passive** voice is often used when one is unsure of the exact identity of the 'doer' of the action, or when one wants to be deliberately evasive about the 'doer'.

> It **has been decided** that ten members of staff will have to forfeit their leave and work over the Christmas period this year.
>
> *(Note that the passive voice means that there is no indication of who made this unpopular decision!)*

4. The **passive** voice is wordy, and often encourages writers to add unnecessary words to sentences.

See: **Wordiness**

14

ACTIVE:	Her notes contain fine illustrations of the weeds and wild flowers found in Namaqualand.
PASSIVE:	Fine illustrations of the weeds and wild flowers found in Namaqualand are contained in her notes.

5. It is best, when writing, to attempt always to use active rather than passive constructions.

See: **Active voice; Passive voice**

Active voice

1. In the active voice, the 'doer' of the action expressed by the verb is the subject of the sentence.

> The boy kicks the ball.

2. In the passive voice, the 'receiver' of the action expressed by the verb is placed in the subject position in the sentence.

> The ball is kicked by the boy.

See: **Active, passive; Passive voice**

Addressing envelopes

1. Three rules apply to addressing envelopes:
   - No punctuation marks
   - Use block format
   - Nothing must appear after the postal code

2. The sequence is as follows:
   Title + Initials + Surname
   Institution

Street address / Postal Box
City
Postal code

Prof S Msimang
Unisa
PO Box 392
Pretoria
0001

Ms V Moodley
7 Peacock Crescent
Laudium
0037

Adjectives

1. Adjectives are modifiers; that is, words that describe, define or limit other words. Adjectives modify nouns and pronouns.

red	happy	big
clever	ridiculous	dirty

2. It is important that adjectives be placed as close as possible to the nouns they modify. The ideal is for the adjective to precede the noun immediately.

the red car	the happy housewife
the big mess	the clever student
the dirty bastard	the ridiculous suggestion

3. Sequence:

More than one adjective can be used to modify a noun. Sequences of more than three adjectives are uncommon, as they sound clumsy. If more than one adjective is used, the adjectives must be ordered in the following sequence:

1. determiner
2. subjective / evaluative adjective (expressing opinion)
3. size or measurement adjective
4. shape adjective
5. condition adjective
6. age adjective
7. colour adjective
8. adjective giving material or origin
9. noun

Obviously, you will want to avoid sequences as long as these!

```
1    2     3     4      5        6    7    8      9
|    |     |     |      |        |    |    |      |
Two ugly small round chipped old blue Dutch plates are all I inherited.
```

4. Derivation:

Adjectives can be derived from other words by adding suffixes. The adjectival suffixes are

-ful	-al	-ible
-able	-y	-ary
-ive	-like	-ic

See: **-able, -ible; Suffixes**

```
beauty + -ful = beautiful
music + -al = musical
act + -ive = active
love + -able = loveable
```

17

5. The present and past participles of verbs can also be used as adjectives.

See: **Participles; Verbs**

the singing nun	the broken plate
the loving husband	the abused child

6. Degrees of Comparison:
   Degrees of comparison allow us to compare the qualities, attributes and features of persons and things. There are three degrees of comparison: Positive, Comparative, and Superlative.

Degree of comparison	Explanation	Form	Example
Positive	The ordinary form of the adjective	Normal	pretty vigorous old
Comparative	Used when comparing two things or persons	adjective + -er OR more + adjective (Use 'more' with adjectives of more than two syllables)	prettier more vigorous older
Superlative	Used when comparing more than two persons or things	adjective + -est OR most + adjective (Use *most* with adjectives of more than two syllables)	prettiest most vigorous oldest

Comparative:
Parents are usually more conservative than their children.
My father is older than my mother.

> Superlative:
> She has three children. The youngest is not yet at school.
> That is the most ridiculous thing I have ever heard!

7. Absolute adjectives:
   There are certain adjectives which are uncomparable. They cannot be used with 'more' or 'most', or with the suffixes '-er' or '-est'. They are **absolute**, and thus, strictly speaking, should not have degrees of comparison. In colloquial speech, however, you may hear degrees of comparison used. (As in 'the most essential thing to remember ...', or 'you seem to be ignoring the most fundamental facts ...'. The degrees of comparison in such cases seem to be serving more as intensifiers used for emphasis than for actual comparison.)

The following adjectives are absolute –

basic	ideal
certain	impossible
chief	obvious
empty	perfect
entire	principal
essential	pure
fatal	unique
final	vital
fundamental	worthless

See: **Modifiers**

Adverbs

1. Adverbs are words that modify verbs, sentences, adjectives, and other adverbs.

Modifying verbs:

He sang **tunelessly**.   She danced **gracefully**.

Modifying sentences:

Certainly, I will help you.
Assuredly, she will pay you tomorrow.

Modifying adjectives:

He was **extremely** helpful.   She was **amazingly** upset.

Modifying other adverbs:

He spoke **very rudely**.   The dog barked **irritatingly loudly**.

Advice, advise, adviser, advisory

1. **Advice** is the noun and refers to the information which is given.
2. **Advise** is the verb and means to give advice.
3. A person who gives advice is called an **adviser**.
4. The adjective **advisory** increasingly influences the spelling of the noun to become 'advisor'. This is wrong, but used widely in South Africa.

See: **Homonyms; Licence, license**

Follow my advice, study hard, and you will pass.
He will advise you to implement my suggestions.
He is an adviser whose opinion is respected.

Affect, effect

1. To avoid confusing these words always use **affect** as a verb, meaning 'to produce an **effect**'.

> How did the weather affect you?

2. Try not to use **affect** as a noun. Synonyms such as 'emotion' or 'feeling' are just as good.

3. Use **effect** as a noun, meaning 'result'.

> What effect did the medicine have on you?

See: **Affective, effective; Homonyms**

Affective, effective

1. **Affective** factors are the emotional factors which can influence an individual in a given situation. Linguists, for example, commonly talk of the influence of **affective** factors on language acquisition.

2. **Effective** means 'having the desired effect' and usually relates to efficient, goal-directed action.

See: **Affect, effect; Homonyms**

Affectation

When applied to a piece of writing **affectation** implies that the writer is trying too hard to impress the reader. Writing that suffers from affectation is generally not very effective as it often uses unnecessary, longer variations of simple words. This often results in meaning being clouded, so that the writing loses its strength.

> X He revised his budgetary estimates upwards.
> √ He increased the amounts in his budget.

See: **Wordiness**

21

Affix

1. An **affix** is a word element added on (or 'fixed on') to a word to change its meaning or its grammatical function.

2. An affix can be added on to the beginning of a word, in which case it is called a **prefix**.

> dis- + illusion = disillusion

3. An affix can be added on to the end of a word, in which case it is called a **suffix**.

> run + -ing = running

See: **Prefixes; Spelling; Suffixes**

Agreement — Pronouns

1. Pronouns must correspond in form to the words which precede them and to which they thus refer. They must agree with their antecedents in person, gender and number.

Person:	Between classes **we** usually go to the cafeteria to eat **our** sandwiches.
	One has to be extremely careful in **one's** writing.
Gender:	**Jane** revised **her** work thoroughly.
	The **dog** hurt **its** foot in trying to jump over the gate.
Number:	The **woman** went on **her** way. The **women** went on **their** way.

2. Words such as the following should always be followed by singular pronouns in formal speech or writing. (In informal speech or writing, 'they' is often used instead.)

   each, every, neither, either, someone, everyone, somebody, anybody, nobody, no-one.

22

> **Everyone** votes according to **his or her** best judgement.
> **Anyone** wishing to have the day off will have to do **his** share of the work.
> **Everyone** should produce **their** own work.

See: **Anybody, anyone; Everybody, everyone, every; Nobody, no-one**

3. Two or more antecedents connected by 'and' take a plural pronoun.

> The teacher and her students went through **their** work carefully.

4. Two or more antecedents in the singular joined by 'or' or 'nor' take a singular pronoun.

> Neither Brian nor Winston will promise to do **his** work.

5. If antecedents joined by 'or' or 'nor' differ in number, the pronoun is determined by the context.

> Neither the foreman nor his men knew what **they** were supposed to do.

6. When there are two antecedents, with one affirmative and the other negative, the pronoun agrees with the affirmative.

> The staff, but not the director, will be paid for **their** overtime work.

See: **Gender; Number; Person**

Agreement — Subject / Verb

1. Each verb must agree with its subject: a subject in the singular thus requires a singular verb, and a subject in the plural

23

requires a plural verb.

> A good speaker **is** usually in great demand.
> Good speakers **are** usually in great demand.

2. A singular subject followed by a phrase containing a plural noun is taken as singular and thus takes a singular verb.

> The noise made by the birds distracts me badly.

3. Subjects connected by 'and' need a plural verb.

> Men and women are not really equal in the eyes of the law.

4. When subjects are joined by 'or' or 'nor' the verb agrees with the nearest subject. Constructions of this nature often seem awkward, and it is better to rephrase them.

> The teacher or the students are wrong.
> The teacher is wrong, or the students are.

5. Indefinite pronouns (such as 'everybody', 'anybody', 'nobody', 'somebody', and so on) always take a singular verb.

> Everybody understands why this should be so.

See: **Anybody, anyone; Everybody, everyone; Nobody, no-one**

6. When one of two subjects is affirmative and the other negative the verb agrees with the affirmative.

> The soldiers, but not the officer, were happy at the thought of leave.

7. Collective nouns are either singular or plural, depending on the context.

> Mathematics is a confusing subject.
> This news is very alarming.
> The scissors are in the desk drawer.

8. Quantities (when used to indicate units), fractions and nouns which are plural in form but singular in meaning are followed by a singular verb.

> Three-quarters of the crop is ruined.
> Four weeks is the approved vacation period.

See: **Antecedent**

Alibi

1. South Africans have been exposed to so many crime detection television programmes that the word **alibi** should be a familiar one to them. Alibi means a claim, or the evidence supporting it, that when an alleged act took place one was elsewhere.

> He says he was alone at home at the time of the murder. No-one saw him reach his home, nobody called him and he can offer no evidence in support of his alibi.

2. The plural form of the word is **alibis**.

3. In informal conversation **alibi** is sometimes used to mean an excuse or a justification. This use is regarded as incorrect in a formal context. A student would not write apologizing to a lecturer for the late submission of a task as follows: 'My alibi for handing my essay in late is that I was ill and could not even find my pen.'

See: **Misused words**

All

1. **All** has many uses. It may be used as an adjective, when it means 'the whole number, extent or amount of'.

> She has lived all her life in Bredasdorp.

2. As an adverb **all** means 'entirely'.

> He was all upset.

3. **All** as a noun is found in some phrases.

> All that I value most.

4. In compounds **all** comes to mean 'without limit'.

> He is an all-round sportsman.

5. When used as a pronoun the meaning of **all** is similar to that which it embodies when it serves as an adjective.

> All are attentive.

6. In each of these instances the word may be used in a range of sentences or phrases each with differing nuances of meaning.

7. Purists argue that **all right**, meaning 'all correct', cannot be used to mean 'good' or 'acceptable' as it would when written *alright.* They demand that one writes – All right (not alright), I'll look into it.

There are also important distinctions between **all together** and **altogether**, **all ready** and **already**, and **all ways** and **always**.

> The students were all together in the hall.
> The hotel's facilities were altogether lacking.
>
> She was all ready to start when the lights went out.
> The shipment had already been sent when the cheque arrived.
>
> The teacher tried all ways of arousing the pupils' interests.
> He always performs in his dress-suit.

Alliteration

1. This is the repetition of consonantal sounds, especially in a line of verse.

2. Alliteration of stressed syllables was the chief metrical device of Old English verse. Since then the device has played a significant role in auditory imagery.

> Whereat, with **b**lade, with **b**loody **b**lameful **b**lade,
> He **b**ravely **b**roached his **b**oiling **b**loody **b**reast-
>
> A Midsummer Night's Dream (V:(i), 148-149)

3. Advertisers and newspapers have become avid users of alliteration because alliterative slogans imprint themselves on our minds.

> The paper for the people
> It washes whiter than white.

See: **Assonance; Consonants**

Allude

1. **Allude**, meaning 'to speak of indirectly', should not be confused with elude - which means 'to escape'.

> In his speech he alluded only briefly to the boy's brave attempt, instead of referring to the matter in great detail.
>
> His meaning eluded me.

See: **Allusion, illusion, delusion**

Allusion, illusion, delusion

1. **Allusion** and **illusion** are often confused. An allusion is a reference to something, and an illusion is something that creates a wrong impression or idea.

> The book contains allusions to early Greek mythology.
>
> The water that we seem to see above the road on a hot day is an optical illusion.

2. **Delusion** is 'a false belief'.

> The man suffers from the delusion that he is the King of England.

3. **Allusive** is the adjective from allusion. It means 'containing allusions or references'.

> His allusive style was very difficult to follow.

4. The adjective from illusion is **illusory**.

5. The adjective **elusive** comes from the verb 'elude' and means 'difficult to find'.

Almost, nearly

1. **Almost** and **nearly** are used for emphasis.

2. **Almost** is used to express feeling or a state of mind.

> I almost wish that I had slapped her face.
> You can almost feel the tension in the country.

3. **Nearly** is used to express the fact that one came near to doing something, but did not.

> I nearly ran over a dog on my way home yesterday.
> I nearly slapped his face.

Alternate, alternative

1. As an adjective **alternate** means 'by turns, first one and then the other'.

> The watering restrictions permit me to use the hose on alternate days: this week I may water the garden on Tuesday, Thursday and Saturday.

2. The adjective **alternative** means 'a choice between two things'.

> An alternative drink to champagne, a non-alcoholic, sparkling grape juice, is now on sale.

3. When used as a noun, **alternative** should be used only when there is the option of one of two choices. However, in informal language, alternative has come to be widely used where there are more than two choices.

> The alternatives were to stay fat, or to eat less.

> Our alternatives are to go to the rugby match, watch the live
> transmission on television, or view the edited version of the
> game tomorrow night.

Ambiguity

1. An **ambiguous** sentence is one with two or more possible
   interpretations, or whose interpretation is in doubt.

2. **Ambiguity** often results from vague pronoun reference, as in
   the following examples.

> Thabo had love and sympathy for everybody, but suddenly he
> began to question them.
> *Does 'them' refer to 'everybody', or to 'love and sympathy'?*
>
> In order to help people you have to understand their problems
> and really care about them.
> *Does 'them' refer to 'people', or to 'their problems'?*
>
> Rajen told Jay that he would be his new boss.
> *Who is the boss, and who the underling?*
>
> My brother has always liked rugby, but I am different.
> This annoys me.
> *What does 'this' refer to? Is it that his brother likes*
> *rugby, or is it rugby itself, or is it the fact that he and his brother*
> *are different?*

See: **Pronouns**

3. Ambiguity can also result from using ambiguous terms. An
   ambiguous term is a term whose meaning is imprecise, often
   because the term is subjectively used, meaning one thing to
   the speaker, but not necessarily the same thing to his or her
   audience.

30

4. Word order can also create ambiguity.

See: **Awkward phrasing; Word order**

American English

1. South African usage tends to follow British usage in matters of spelling, idiom and construction, although in the sciences and popular culture there is a move towards American terminology.

2. A commonly noticed difference in spelling is the tendency for American spelling to drop the 'u' in words ending in '-our' ('behaviour' - 'behavior'; 'honour' - 'honor'). Most dictionaries will indicate American spellings with the abbreviation US. American spelling would generally be regarded as a spelling error in South African contexts. However, if quoting directly from an American text, you should retain the original spelling and not 'correct' it.

3. American English also has a number of vocabulary differences, many of which we have subconsciously absorbed from television and the cinema. (Think about 'elevator' vs 'lift', and 'sidewalk' vs 'pavement', for example). It is not practicable to provide a full list here, but it is well to remember that considerable differences do exist, and that one cannot therefore assume that communication between a South African English speaker and an American English speaker will always be easy or automatic.

See: **Practice, practise; Program, programme**

Among, amongst

1. Where you have a comparison between two objects or people, use **between**; where the number is greater than two, use **among**.

> The seed fell among stones.

2. **Amongst** is an alternative form of among, although 'among' is preferred in South African English.

Am

See: **Anomalous finite verbs**

Amount, number

1. Both **amount** and **number** are used to refer to a quantity of something.

2. **Amount** can only be used to refer to uncountable nouns.

> an amount of rice
> an amount of sand
> an amount of love

3. **Number** can only be used to refer to countable nouns.

> a number of people
> a number of teabags
> a number of animals

See: **Nouns**

Ampersand (&)

1. The ampersand – & – is a sign for 'and'. It should only be used in names of firms.

> Rightford, Searle, Tripp & Makin

2. In all other writing 'and' should be used.

See: **And**

An

1. **An** is the form of the indefinite article used before words beginning with a vowel or an unsounded h.

	an advocate	an eland	an heir
	an hour	an impi	
BUT	a hare	a hair	a horse

2. Because the consonant 'S' is pronounced 'ess', **an** will be used before abbreviations such as 'SAA', 'SANDF' and so on.

	An SAA pilot An SABC programme
	An SAP spokesperson
BUT	A South African Airways pilot
	A South African Broadcasting Corporation programme
	A South African Police Services spokesperson

See: **A; Articles**

Analogy, analogous

1. An analogy points to features of similarity between two things which in other respects are unalike.

> A student is to knowledge as a sponge is to water.

2. Analogies may be brief or lengthy, but the resemblance between the concepts in an analogy must be one that illuminates the relationship the writer wishes to convey.

3. All metaphors and similes are based on analogy.

See: **Metaphor; Simile**

4. The adjective is 'analogous' and is spelt with only two a's. The word means 'similar or parallel to'.

And

1. **And** is a coordinating conjunction.

See: **Conjunctions**

2. **And** joins expressions with equal weight, and which are grammatically similar.

Nouns:	bread and cheese
Verbs:	They sang and danced until dawn.
Clauses:	The left-wingers want one thing, and the right-wingers want another.

3. In joining more than two expressions, **and** is usually put before the last expression.

> We drank, talked, and danced.
> I wrote the letters, Bongi addressed them, and Tsepo posted them.

4. **And** is not usually used to link adjectives before a noun, although **and** is used when the adjectives refer to different parts of the same thing.

	√ Thank you for your nice long letter.
	X Thank you for your nice and long letter.
BUT	a blue and green jersey
	a wood and metal table

Anglicized words

These are words taken from other languages and which, through use, have become part of the English vocabulary. As a rule, an anglicized word which appears in a reputable dictionary is acceptable in formal writing.

apartheid	stoep	ubuntu	bakkie
toyi-toyi	braai	muti	

See: **South Africanisms, Toyi-toyi**

Anomalous finite verbs

1. The following verbs are classified as anomalous finite verbs:

Present Tense	Past Tense
am is are	was were
can	could
dare	dared
do does	did
have has	had
may	might
must	—
need	—
ought	—
shall	should
—	used
will	would

2. Unlike regular verbs, anomalous finite verbs form their negatives by adding the word *not*, or its contraction -n't, after the verb.

35

> I am not happy.
> You mustn't allow that to happen.

3. Some of these anomalous finite verbs are also used as ordinary verbs. **Dare** means 'to be courageous or brave enough, to face, or to challenge'.

> They would not dare to be so rude.
> I dare you to dive off the cliff into the river.

Do means 'to perform or carry out some action'.

> Do the work at once.
> Did you do as I asked?

Have means 'to take, accept, obtain or receive'.

> What shall we have for breakfast?
> I will have ice in my drink, please.

Need means 'to want or require'.

> Does she need our assistance?
> This essay needs rewriting.

4. Questions are formed by using the helping or auxiliary verbs 'do', 'does' or 'did' in combination with regular verbs. By contract, the anomalous finite verbs begin questions and do not require the helping verb, 'do'.

> Do you ever visit the beerhall?
> Do you want to borrow my bakkie to transport your furniture?
>
> BUT   I am going. (*Becomes*: Am I going?)
> He can play golf well. (*Becomes*: Can he play golf well?)

5. In order to form a negative statement, the auxiliary verb 'do', together with the word 'not', is used with a regular verb.

> He braais the meat. (*Becomes*: He does not braai the meat.)
>
> She swallowed the witchdoctor's muti. (*Becomes*: She did not swallow the witchdoctor's muti.)

6. Negative questions are formed by using anomalous finite verbs and the contraction 'n't' with regular verbs.

> Don't spiders eat their own kind?
> Won't you have to live in a pondokkie?

7. Anomalous finite verbs are also used for tag-questions.

> You are playing, aren't you?
> She must do it, mustn't she?

8. Brief answers to questions make use of anomalous finite verbs without the verb contained in the question.

> Have you climbed this koppie before? Yes, I have.
> Are you selling any spanspek? No, I am not.

Antecedent

An antecedent is generally a noun, clause or sentence to which a following pronoun or relative pronoun refers.

> Knives, which are sharp, are dangerous in the hands of children.
> *Knives is the antecedent of which.*

See: **Agreement – Pronouns**

Antonyms

Antonyms are words of opposite meaning.

> Dark is an antonym of light.
> Pretty is an antonym of ugly.

See: **Opposites; Synonyms**

Anybody, anyone

1. **Anybody** and **anyone** are both pronouns which refer to any person.

2. These pronouns are singular, and in formal usage any pronoun or possessive referring to them should be singular. In colloquial use, the pronoun 'they' is more commonly used. These pronouns also take a singular verb.

> Has anyone a stapler he can lend me?
> Would anybody in his right mind believe such a thing?
>
> Colloquial:
> Has anyone a stapler they can lend me?
> Would anybody in their right mind believe such a thing?

3. **Any one** (two words) means 'whichever one (person or thing)

38

you choose'. It is used to emphasize the fact that only one single person or thing is meant.

> Any one of us could have made the same mistake.
>
> Join the Book of the Month Club, and we will send you any one of these lavishly illustrated books absolutely free!

4. **Nobody** and **no-one** are also singular and thus take singular pronouns and verbs.

> No-one is to leave the room.
> Nobody enjoys being criticized by his friends.
>
> Colloquial:
> Nobody enjoys being criticized by their friends.

5. **Everyone** and **everybody** are also singular pronouns, and the same rules apply. **Every one** (two words) is used to emphasize each individual member of a group of things or people, as is the word **each**.

> Every one of these typewriters needs repair.
> Each one of these students will receive a diploma.

6. Currently, the pressure of avoiding sexist bias in one's language has lead to an increasing acceptance of the colloquial use of the plural 'they' and 'their' to refer to words like 'anyone', 'no-one' and 'everyone', in preference to the masculine pronouns 'he' and 'his'.

> In case of fire, everyone must take their belongings and leave their hotel rooms as rapidly as possible.

See: **Agreement; Everybody, everyone, every; Nobody, no-one**

Apostrophe (')

The apostrophe has four uses:

1. To indicate where letters have been left out of contractions.
   (Contractions should be avoided in formal writing.)

   > do + not = don't
   > she + is = she's
   > it + is = it's
   > we + are = we're

2. To indicate the possessive form of a noun:

   > South Africa's constitution
   > The men's cars

   In cases where the word ends in '-s' (as in girls, Jones, states)
   the possessive '-s' is dropped, and an apostrophe merely
   placed on its own at the end of the word.

   > The girls' dresses
   > Jones' letter
   > the independent states' leaders

   Possessive pronouns do not take an apostrophe.

   > The book is hers.
   > He delivered his speech this morning.
   > The dog is very possessive about its bowl.

3. The apostrophe is used to write the plural form of a word
   which does not normally have a plural form:

> You should mind your p's and q's.
> Children are confused by too many do's and don't's.

4. Apostrophes indicate when the shortened form of a word or date is being used.

> 1999 – '99
> influenza – 'flu
> refrigerator – 'fridge
> telephone – 'phone
> *The last two have become common usage, and thus are often written without the apostrophe.*

See: **Possessive case**

Articles

1. A part of speech, articles are adjectives. They modify the items to which they refer by either limiting them or making them more exact. There are two types of articles: definite and indefinite.

2. Indefinite articles:
   A and **an** indicate a single but unspecified item.

> There is a bar in almost every hotel.
> There is also an off-sales attached to each hotel.

3. Definite article:
   The indicates one particular person or thing.

> The skokiaan he brewed was much stronger than beer.

4. Use **a** before words beginning with a consonant sound (a tokoloshe, a vastrap, a Unisa student), and **an** before words

41

beginning with a vowel sound (an aloe, an uncle).

5. The following guidelines are useful.

- Proper nouns seldom take articles.

> Gauteng   Desmond Tutu   Waterberg Motors

- Use **a** before abbreviations which begin with letters having a consonant sound.

> a WO seal   (a wine-of-origin seal)

- Use **an** before abbreviations which begin with letters having a vowel sound.

> an IFP meeting

See: **A; An**

- In a title capitalise an article only if it is the first word.

> An Examination of the World's Recession in a Decade of Turmoil.

- Do not omit all articles from your writing, as a telegraphic style makes the reading more difficult.

> X Send letter to manager
> √ Send a letter to the manager.

- Abstractions take articles only when followed by a phrase or clause.

> What is honour? This is love.
> It is the honour attached to the work that attracts her.
> His is the love of an unselfish man.

See: **A; An; The**

As

1. **As** is a conjunction. It can be used to give a reason.

> As it is raining today, I will have to postpone doing the washing until tomorrow.

2. **As** can be used to express the function of a person or object.

> He worked as a waiter while studying for his degree.
> Perlemoen shells are often used as ashtrays.

3. **As** is used to express similarity. While 'like' is used before nouns and pronouns, **as** is used before clauses and prepositional phrases.

> Do as I say, not as I do.
> In Johannesburg, as in other big cities, peak hour traffic congestion is a major problem.
> She dances as lightly as a feather.
> She dances as if inspired.
> BUT She dances like a born ballerina.

See: **Like**

Assonance

The term identifies the repetition of stressed vowel sounds, which are similar or almost similar. This repetition is not accompanied by the agreement of consonant sounds as this would make a rhyme.

> The merry bells ring,
> To welcome the Spring.
>
> 'The Echoing Green' by William Blake

See: **Alliteration; Rhyme**

Audience (reader or listener)

1. Speech or writing should always be appropriate to the audience; that is, the person or people with whom one is in conversation, or one's readers.

2. For example, while slang, colloquialisms and swear words may be appropriate in an informal context (a party with friends, or a personal letter), a more formal register is required in most writing and in conversation with one's superiors.

See: **Register**

3. When writing it is extremely important to keep your audience in mind. Who are they? What are their expectations of you? What do you need to achieve by writing to them? The following checklist could help you write more effectively. Answer the questions before embarking on any piece of writing.

Audience Checklist	
1.	What is your subject?
2.	Who is going to read your essay / article / report / memo? (Who are your prospective readers?)
3.	What's the best thing you can say about your readers?
4.	What's the worst thing you can say about your readers?
5.	What do you think is your readers' top priority in a piece

of writing? (ie What do you think they're looking for,
above all else?)
6.	How much do your readers know about your topic?
7.	How do you want your readers to feel when they have
finished reading what you have written?
8.	How can you make them feel that way?
9.	What is the main point that you want to make to your
readers?
10.	Complete the sentence: If nothing else, I want my
readers to understand that / how / why........ .

Autobiography

1. An autobiography is a person's recounting of the story of his
or her own life, with the emphasis on the author's developing
personality and character. An example is Nelson Mandela's
Long Walk to Freedom.

2. Memoirs, on the other hand, emphasize the people known and
the events witnessed during the author's life.

See: **Biography**

Auxiliary verbs

1. Auxiliary verbs are 'helping' verbs used with other verbs to
perform specific grammatical functions and express certain
meanings.

2. Do, be, have: These three words have specific grammatical
functions.
   Do is used to make negative statements, to ask questions, and
   for emphasis with the simple present and simple past tenses.

	I enjoy studying
Negative:	I do not enjoy studying.
Emphasis:	I do enjoy studying.
Question:	Do you enjoy studying?

Be forms are used with the present and past participles of verbs to make the progressive tenses and passives.

> He is studying the report.
> The report was studied by the manager.

Have is used to make perfect tense forms.

> He has done the work.
> I have read the book.
> He had compiled the report by last Friday.

See: **Anomalous finite verbs**

Auxiliary verbs — Modal auxiliaries

1. Modal auxiliaries include:

can	could	may	might
will	would	shall	should
ought	must need		

2. Modal auxiliaries do not take the third person singular '-s', and do not have infinitives.

3. Modal auxiliaries are used to express the following meanings:
   • Obligation - should ought must

> You should always be polite.   You ought to respond to his letters.
> You must read this book – it's very good.

- Certainty – shall   will   must   can't

> I shall be in Cape Town next week.
> Everything will turn out for the best.
> You must be exhausted!
> I knew when I met him that I would end up marrying him.
> You can't be tired, you've slept all day!

- Probability – should   ought to   may

> I should be home by five o'clock
> It ought to be in order if you submit your assignment a day or two late.
> It may be hot enough to swim.

- Weak probability – might   could

> I might not be home in time for supper.
> We could finish this tomorrow, I suppose.

- Theoretical possibility – can

> How many pizzas can you eat at one sitting?
> It can be very cold in Gauteng in winter.

- Conditional possibility – would   could   might

> I would help you, if I had the time.
> I could meet you in town, unless you would prefer to come out to my office.
> I might be able to finish this work by lunchtime, provided that I'm not interrupted.

See: **Can, may; May, might; Shall, will**

Awful, awfully

1. **Awful** originally meant 'full of awe', inspiring respect tinged with fear. With words such as 'terribly', 'horribly', and 'frightfully', **awfully** is colloquially applied to situations which contain no awe, terror, horror, or fright.

2. Sentences such as 'You've been most awfully kind' should be avoided, not only for their phoniness, but because the meaning of the word has been degraded and its use is therefore ineffective.

See: **Misused words**

Awkward phrasing

Awkward phrasing results from an inversion of the normal order of words in an English sentence. Awkward phrasing interferes with ease of reading and can distort meaning.

1. Ambiguous order
Ensure that there is a clear relationship between modifying words, phrases, or clauses and the elements they modify.

> X There is a panel discussion tonight about drug addiction in the school hall.
> √ Tonight there is a panel discussion in the school hall about drug addiction.
>
> X Who is the woman dancing with the manager in the low cut dress?
> √ Who is the woman in the low cut dress dancing with the manager?

2. Awkward separation of elements
Avoid unnecessary separation of a subject and its verb, a verb and its object or complement, or the parts of a verb.

X My boss, after considering what the trip would cost and how long it would take, refused to let me go.

Awkward separation of subject and verb.

√ After considering what the trip would cost and how long it would take, my boss refused to let me go.

X The evidence shows, if you examine it careful and impartially, that advertising on television achieves the best results.

Awkward separation of verb and object.

√ A careful and impartial examination of the evidence shows that television advertising achieves the best results.

X We have since then had no more trouble.

Awkward separation of verb parts.

√ We have had no more trouble since then.

B

Bathos

Bathos is the use of anticlimax. It is a descent from the dignified and dramatic to the mundane. It is sometimes used for a deliberately ludicrous effect, but can also be the unintentional result of not ordering or selecting one's points.

> Today was the worst day of my life. My husband wrote his car off in an accident. I was summonsed for R5 000 in outstanding traffic fines, and, to top it all, I broke three fingernails.

Begging the question

This is a trap into which inexperienced writers blunder, and refers to the process of assuming that an argument (or something under examination) has already been proved. Thus, if a botanist were to say 'As it is possible that the leaves could become yellow, we shall have to look for a way of preventing this', she would be begging the question: namely, what if they do not become yellow?

Beside, besides

1. **Beside** is today most often used as a preposition, meaning 'by the side of' and 'at the end of one's self-control'.

> He stood beside me in the queue.
> He was beside himself with rage.

2. **Besides** is also used as a preposition, meaning 'in addition to' and 'except, excluding'.

> Besides all this, between you and us there is a great gulf.
> What else have you done, besides making a mess?

Between

1. Like 'among', **between** is concerned with relationships. Because between is a preposition it takes an object.

> Between you and me, I think he is a fool.
> Please share the food equally between you and him.
> Share the sweets between the two of us.

2. Notice that, unlike 'among', **between** refers to only two objects, people, or phenomena.

See: **Among, amongst**

Biannual, biennial

1. A **biennial** is a plant which lives for two years. A **biennial** meeting is one which occurs once every two years.

2. A **biannual** journal is published twice a year.

3. Avoid confusion by writing 'half-yearly' or 'twice a year', and 'two years' or 'every other year'.

Bibliography

1. A bibliography is a list of books, articles, essays, or other sources of information arranged alphabetically according to the author's surname.

2. A working bibliography is a set of note cards identifying works consulted in the course of writing or research.

3. A final bibliography is a list placed at the end of the written work.

See: **Footnotes; Plagiarism; Referencing**

Biography

A biography is an account of the life of a person (not the author), setting out his or her background and milieu; events, experiences and achievements in his or her life; and the development of his/her character.

See: **Autobiography**

Bioscope

See: **Cinema**

Borrow

One borrows something from someone else, on the understanding that it is to be returned.

> May I borrow your book? I'll give it back to you tomorrow.

See: **Lend**

Both ... and

1. **Both ... and** are correlative conjunctions. That is, they join two related items.

2. **Both** can not be used when more than two items are being corre-lated. The two items correlated should be of the same kind.

> **Both** + adjective + **and** + adjective
> He is both intelligent and handsome.
>
> **Both** + noun + **and** + noun
> South Africans, both athletes and spectators, were banned
> from the 1988 Olympic Games.
>
> **Both** + clause + **and** + clause
> He both plays rugby and takes ballet lessons.

See: **Correlative conjunctions**

3. **Both ... and** cannot join full sentences.

Brackets [], parentheses ()

1. Brackets **[...]**, which should not be confused with parentheses **(...)**, are used to indicate unquoted material in a quotation.

> 'Almost 19 percent [of the people] are from Durban, and
> 24 percent [of the travellers] are from Cape Town.'

2. Parentheses **(...)** are used to indicate explanatory material and additional material within a sentence. (Note: the plural form 'parentheses' is used because these punctuation marks always come in pairs. A single one is called a 'parenthesis'.)

> Port Elizabeth (the friendly city) is the port through which our
> wool is exported.

3. When parentheses occur at the end of a sentence, the punctuation is placed after the last parenthesis.

> Our wool is exported through Port Elizabeth
> (often referred to as 'the friendly city').

4. When a complete sentence is placed within parentheses, the full-stop comes before the last parenthesis.

> Fugard is one of South Africa's finest dramatists.
> (There have, of course, been other dramatists of stature.)

5. Numbers which help to indicate the logic of a sentence should also be placed within parentheses.

> Aspirant writers need
> (1) to know the difference between brackets and parentheses,
> (2) to use parentheses circumspectly; and
> (3) to follow the rules of punctuation closely.

Brevity

While one's writing should always be as concise as possible, care should be taken that no essential information is omitted. Therefore, check that all necessary facts have been included before pruning the work by eliminating superfluous adjectives and adverbs, and by checking that as many active verbs as possible have been used. Good writing is marked by the use of full and proper sentences: thus beware of falling into the habit of employing telegraphese - which is the type of writing found in telegrams.

See: **Active, passive; Business writing; Passive constructions; Wordiness**

Budget

1. To **budget** is to estimate probable future income and expenditure as realistically as possible.

2. The spelling of the transitive verb and intransitive verb forms often cause difficulty. They are derived by adding only the suffixes -*ed* or -*ing*.

> Cherie has budgeted for the purchase of a new bicycle next year.
>
> Budgeting is not an exact science, but one tries to foresee what patterns of income and expenditure are likely to occur.

See: **Spelling**

Business writing

The writing we do in business needs to be concise, to the point, and to contain all information relevant to the matter at hand. The following guidelines are useful in this regard:

1. Business **letters** should always be typed. The proper form of a business letter should be used (see Letter writing). The first paragraph of a business letter should refer specifically to the matter at hand.

See: **Curriculum vitae**

2. A **resumé** is a summary of your background and work experience. Keep it short: no more than one page. Include only the most important information, and emphasise your strong points.

3. **Letters of enquiry** are designed to obtain information. State your needs clearly so that your reader will know what you want.

Paragraph 1:   Give your reasons for writing.

Paragraph 2:   Provide details of what you need.

Paragraph 3:   Thank the reader and, if necessary, specify the period within which you need to have the information or materials requested.

4. **Responses to letters of enquiry** should provide all the information requested: if this is not available, an explanation will be necessary.

5. In **letters of complaint** you should be firm and reasonable, rather than threatening or sarcastic. Explain your position concisely. Businesses do not have time for long, wordy essays.

See: **Letter writing**

6. A **memorandum (memo)** is a message which circulates within an institution. If yours does not have its own printed forms, you could copy the format used in the example below.

Several points about memorandums are worth noting:

- There is no need to have formal salutations and greetings such as are needed in letters directed outside of the organization.

- The style is direct and to the point. In this respect it is similar to a business letter.

- In this case, the printed memo provides all the information such as the originating department so that only the parts presented in script need to be inserted each time.

- The author signs the memorandum at the end of the text.

ZIPPO UNLEADED PETROL DISTRIBUTORS
National Sales Division

MEMORANDUM

To: Ms M Bags   Ref: 97/28
        Head, Finance Division
From: J B Mahlangu
        Head, National Sales Division
Date: 97/02/15

Image of our Company

I know that you will be as concerned as I am to read the attached copy of a letter that was sent to our biggest Zippo Customer Outlet in Gauteng. As you know this outlet accounts for no less than 8% of our Group's total sales. The image that our Group presents is very important if we are to retain the confidence of our key clients. This is not made easier when a routine issue of a slightly delayed payment results in a letter such as the one in question.

I am sure that it is right that we write and remind them of the outstanding balance, but my problem is with the care with which the letter has been written. There are only three sentences, yet they contain five errors. There are two major sentence construction errors, two spelling mistakes (which any spelling checker in a word processor would have picked up) and a major usage error.

I believe we need to ensure that all of our routine letters are carefully scrutinized so as to ensure that they all leave an impression of professionalism, correctness and efficiency.

I do hope that you will take this concern up with your staff and help us to ensure that our profit margins continue to grow.

encl.
JBM/typ/

But

1. **But** is used as a coordinating conjunction and as a preposition.

2. As a conjunction **but** is used to contrast two statements.

> I searched through every cupboard for my knobkierie, but I
> could not find it.

3. The use of a comma before **but** depends on the length of the pause needed by the context.

4. When used as a preposition (meaning 'except' or 'excluding') **but** is followed by the object form.

> They are all going but me.

See: **Conjunctions; Prepositions**

C

Can, may

1. **Can** is used to express general ability. Strictly speaking, the sentence

    'Dad, can I use the car tonight?'

   means 'Dad, am I physically able to use the car tonight?'

2. In asking for permission, **may** should be used.

> 'May I borrow your stapler?'
> 'Yes, if you can find it.'
>
> 'Dad, may I use the car tonight?'

See: **Auxiliary verbs; May, might**

Canon

This word has several meanings:

1. **Canon** law is the law of the Church.

2. The principle or standard by which something is judged is often referred to as its **canon**.

> the canons of good taste

3. **Canon** also describes a body of writings accepted as genuine.

> For a time King John was not included in the Shakespeare canon.

4. A **canon** may be an official list of, for example, Roman Catholic saints. It is also the title of a priest who performs duties in a cathedral.

5. **Canon** must not be confused with 'cannon' which refers to a large, heavy piece of artillery.

Capital letters

1. Capital letters are used at the beginning of every English sentence.

> A mealie has become a delicacy in drought-stricken areas.

2. Direct speech also always begins with a capital letter, even when the utterance does not begin the sentence.

> She frowned slightly before declaring, 'We think that this foolishness has gone on long enough'.

3 The pronoun 'I' is always written with a capital as are the terms of address 'Father' and 'Mother'. 'Uncle' and 'Aunt' are written with capitals when they are used in combination with names.

>   'Father, Mother and I are going to town now.'
>   Uncle Jonas and Aunt Mirriam have gone on holiday.
> BUT   I told my mother and father of my plans.
>   My uncle and aunt live in Mpumalanga.

4. All names or proper nouns begin with capital letters.

> Nelson Mandela   Freedom Square
> Soweto   Bafana Bafana

Orange River	Kwazulu-Natal
Zimbabwe	Iron Age
Renaissance	Second World War
Government of National Unity	Christianity
Roman Catholic Church	Parliament
Shakespearean	

5. When the word church is used as a name (referring to the institution in general) it takes a capital letter.
When the word is used to refer to a building, a capital letter is not used.

> The Church is a strong advocate of reform.
> BUT The roof of our church leaks badly.

6. When a point of the compass forms part of a placename, use a capital letter.

> South Africa   Western Australia   Far East

7. In the titles of books, poems, journals, music, films and articles or essays, the first word and main words are given capital letters.

> *The South African Handbook of Grammar, Style, and Usage*
> 'Lament for a Dead Cow'
> *South African Journal of Higher Education*
> 'Rock Around the Clock'
> *Cry the Beloved Country*

8. Capitals are also used for titles or rank.

President Mandela	Chief Justice
Bishop of Johannesburg	Vice-Chancellor
Managing Director	General

9. With a few exceptions lines of verse begin with capital letters.

> In Xanadu did Kubla Khan
> A stately pleasure-dome decree:
> Where Alph, the sacred river, ran
> Through caverns measureless to man
> Down to a sunless sea ...
>
> From 'Kubla Khan' by Samuel Taylor Coleridge;

10. It has been customary practice to capitalise all references to the Deity, although an increasingly accepted modern practice is that pronouns for the Deity are not written with capitals.

	In the name of the Father, and of the Son and of the Holy Ghost, amen.		
ALSO	Allah	Almighty	Christ
	Jehovah	Lord	Holy
	Trinity	Yahweh	

11. Brand names and registered trademarks are also capitalised.

Coca Cola	Kodak	Aspro
Opel	Iwisa Mealiemeal	Jungle Oats

Case

The case of nouns or pronouns indicates subjects,

complements or modifiers.

1. With regard to nouns, the matter is fairly simple:
   • The subject is placed first, before the verb.
   • Complements appear after the verb or preposition they are completing.
   • The possessive case is formed by adding an apostrophe and (usually) an 's'.

2. Pronouns are a little more difficult; perhaps because they are used more often than nouns:

Case	Pronoun	
Subjective	I	we
	you	
	he, she, it	they
Object / Complement	me	us
	you	
	him, her, it	them
Reflexive	myself	ourselves
	yourself	
	himself, herself, itself	themselves
Possessive	my	our
	your	
	his, hers, its	theirs

• Use the subjective case for a subjective complement.

This is he.

• After 'than' or 'as' use the subjective case.

> He is as clever as I. *(Implied: He is as clever as I am.)*

• Use the case demanded by the function of the pronoun when words are used in pairs.

> The prize was presented to him and me.
> He and I will be at the party.

• When a pronoun is modified by a gerund, use the possessive case.

> He was very irritated by my coughing.

• The subject of an infinitive takes the objective case.

> They thought him to be the best director in the company

See also **Who, whom, whose, who's**

Catharsis

When used in its literary sense, catharsis refers to a 'cleansing' of the emotions through feelings of extreme pity or fear. It is most commonly used in respect of the literary genre known as tragedy.

See: **Tragedy**

Cinema

The terms cinema and bioscope are both acceptable, although 'bioscope' has become very dated. The terms 'movies', 'flicks' (or 'flieks'), however, are colloquial English and should not be used in formal situations. In departments of English or Communications, one may find the terms 'film' and 'film studies' being used.

Classicism

1. **Classicism** is used to describe adherence to the classical style of literature or art.

2. A **classicist** conforms, in his writing, to the rules or models of ancient Greece and Rome.

3. The classic style is realistic, simple, rational, harmonious, regular and restrained. Simply put, it is the opposite of romanticism.

See: **Romanticism**

Clause

1. A clause is a group of words containing a subject and a verb.

2. An **independent clause** (as the adjective implies) is a clause that can stand on its own, and that makes sense on its own. Independent clauses can be linked without losing their independence.

> The dog barked.
> The cat ran away.
>
> The dog barked and the cat ran away.

3. A **dependent clause** does not make complete sense on its own, and has to be linked to a main clause. Dependent clauses add to the meaning of the sentences which contain them.

There are three main types of dependent clauses:
• Noun Clauses act as nouns in sentences.

> Do you know **what the answer is**?

• Adjectival clauses describe nouns.

> He is a rugby players **who is notorious for his rudeness to the press**.

- Adverbial clauses describe verbs.

> The accident happened **where construction workers were busy widening the highway**.

4. A dependent clause standing on its own is known as a fragmentary sentence.

> who were the first to arrive

Clichés

1. The word 'cliché' comes from the French. The literal meaning is 'a stereotype'. It originally meant a metal plate cast from a mould used to produce large numbers of identical copies. In English, a cliché means an expression or phrase which has become meaningless and ineffective through overuse.

2. Clichés are trite, hackneyed, and threadbare expressions which create a tired, stale and flabby impression when used in writing. It is not coincidental that clichés are also called 'dead metaphors'.

3. Some clichés 'to avoid like the plague' are:

Avoid like the plague	Beat about the bush
Bored stiff	Bright and early
Crystal clear	Dead as a doornail
Don't count your chickens	Feast your eyes on
Fits like a glove	Going all out to win
Hook, line, and sinker	Horses for courses
Kill two birds with one stone	Last but not least

Levelling the playing fields
Live and let live
More or less
Nip in the bud
Pass the buck
Pull your socks up
Reading between the lines
Short and sweet
Sober as a judge
Thick as thieves
Water over the dam
Year in and year out

Lock, stock and barrel
Mind over matter
Mountains out of molehills
Nose to the grindstone
Put your foot down
Raining cats and dogs
Safe and sound
Sigh of relief
Stiff upper lip
Too numerous to mention
Without rhyme or reason

4. There are numerous others, many of them, unfortunately 'drummed into' children's heads at school (as free as ...? as white as ...?).

5. New expressions can rapidly become clichés for a time. 'Crossing the Rubicon', for example, became a cliché during the PW Botha years. It is very possible that 'transparency' and the 'rainbow nation' will be the clichés of 'the New South Africa' (a term which is itself becoming a cliché!).

6. Writers who wish to communicate clearly, vividly, and forcefully will avoid using clichés 'at all costs'.

Clumsy expression

This is any construction that does not clearly convey your meaning to the reader. In order to ensure that your writing is clear, it is useful to proofread your work by reading aloud: often you will 'hear' a clumsy expression before you see it.

See: **Awkward phrasing**

Collective nouns

1. A collective noun means a group or collection of people, places, things, actions, concepts or qualities.

67

A flock of sheep or birds	a drove of oxen
a flight of pigeons	a herd of cattle
a pack of cards	a plague of locusts
a pride of lions	a school of porpoises
a swarm of bees	a litter of puppies
an army of soldiers	a board of directors
a congregation of church members	
a crew of a ship	a fleet of ships
an orchard of fruit-trees	a team of soccer-players.

2. Collective nouns take singular verbs unless they are used to refer to the individuals and not the group.

> My family is going to live in Cape Town.
> The jury is deliberating on the case.
> BUT The team are individualists.
> *(This usage is less common.)*

3. Certain collective nouns, such as crowd, group or number, are usually followed by a plural noun in a possessive phrase. The consequence is that the verb takes a plural form.

> A crowd of spectators have squeezed into the ground.
> A group of visitors are entering the hospital.
> A number of students are going to pass.

See: **Nouns**

Colloquialisms

Colloquialisms are generally more appropriate to spoken than written English. As written English is more formal than spoken English, you should try to avoid using colloquial words. Your dictionary will help you here by marking such words with the abbreviation *coll.*

jerk (as a noun)
cool (as in 'real cool)
kids
plain talk
crack down
okay

Colon (:)

1. A colon – : – is a mark of punctuation. It indicates a pause almost as long as a full-stop.

2. Colons are used to introduce a list, an explanation, a speech, a quotation, or a definition. In titles, a colon may be used to separate a main heading from a division.

Ingredients: Sugar, cornflour, glucose, milk solids, cocoa, butter.
The woman shrieked: 'Stop him! He's got a bomb in his suitcase!'
Punctuation: The Comma
Zodwa will not be at work today: apparently she has caught pneumonia.

See: **Punctuation**

Comedy

1. The opposite of a tragedy, a comedy is a drama which has a happy ending and which deals with everyday life and humorous or amusing events.

2. A musical comedy is a production with music, songs and dancing, which treats a theme lightly.

3. Some of the classic comedies, while serious plays, show life in such a form that their impact on the audience is neither painful nor tragic.

Comma (,)

A comma is a form of punctuation used to mark off sentences with short pauses. The following are the most common uses of the comma:

1. Commas are used to separate items on a list.

> I attended meetings in Pretoria, Johannesburg, Cape Town and Durban.

2. Commas are used to separate clauses, in order to indicate where the reader should pause.

> Table Mountain, which is often covered with a 'tablecloth' of cloud, is one of the major scenic attractions in Cape Town.

3. Commas are used to separate adverbs when these intrude in a sentence.

> The manager, surprisingly, insisted on making his own coffee.

Commas should NOT be used in the following cases.

1. Commas are NOT used before reported speech clauses.

> X He said, that he was happy to be there.
> X I wonder, if I should go.

2. Commas are NOT used in cases where the clause is essential to give the subject a clear meaning (an identifying relative clause).

> X He said, that he was happy to be there.
> X I wonder, if I should go.
> X The woman, in the red dress, is the one you spoke to.

3. Commas are NOT used between two grammatically complete sentences where a full-stop is possible. This error is known as a comma splice. (In such cases rather use a full-stop or a semi-colon.)

> X I always eat too much at staff tea parties, milk tart is my particular weakness.

See: **Comma splice**

Comma splice

1. Make it a rule not to use a comma unless you have a specific reason for using one. Above all, do not use a comma to separate independent sentences in a compound sentence that has no connective word between the two parts. If you do, a comma splice will be formed.

> X In English 1, students meet once a week in small groups, this gives them a chance to discuss their work.
>
> X The tutor continued to discuss the basic rules of punctuation, nobody informed her that the period had ended.
>
> RATHER
>
> √ In English 1, students meet once a week in small groups. This gives them a chance to discuss their work.
>
> √ The tutor continued to discuss the basic rules of punctuation. Nobody informed her that the period had ended.

2. If two independent sentences are joined without any

punctuation at all, the error would be termed a run-together, or fused sentence.

See: **Comma; Fused sentences**

Comment

Some South African politicians have difficulty in the pronunciation of this word which may function as a noun or verb. (It is particularly common in the phrase 'No comment' and the sentence 'I would like / not like to comment on that at this stage.') Reputable dictionaries, other than those which document American pronunciation, are unanimous: the stress is on the first syllable which is pronounced similarly to the first syllable of that other favourite political term, 'communism'. The phonetic transcription is 'kʌment. The second syllable rhymes with 'bent'.

Comparative adjectives

See: **Adjectives (Degrees of Comparison); Comparison**

Comparison

1. A comparison is made when the extent of similarities and differences between people or things is determined.

2. Similes and metaphors are figurative comparisons.

See: **Analogy; Metaphor; Simile**

3. Adjectives have three degrees of comparison.

Positive	Comparative	Superlative
good	better	best
old	older	oldest
bright	brighter	brightest

Positive:

As a South African city, Pretoria is growing fast.

Comparative:

As a South African city, Pretoria is growing faster than any other.

Superlative:

As a South African City, Pretoria is growing the fastest.

See: **Adjectives**

Complement, compliment

These two words are often needlessly confused. A good rule of thumb is to link **complement** with 'complete' or 'completion' (the first six letters are similar). This will help to serve as a reminder that **compliment** is related to praise.

His research, which complemented *(added to, rounded off)* the work of his colleagues, was complimented *(praised)* by the director.

Compound words

A compound word is a word made up of two or more words to form a single new word, which may be written as one word, or hyphenated. Compounds can be formed in the following ways:

1. Noun + prepositional phrase

mother-in-law

The plural of this kind of compound word is customarily made by adding an '-s' to the noun, not to the whole word.

See: **Plurals**

2. Noun + noun

mineworker	wrongdoer	bookmaker

3. Adjective + adjective

Anglo-Zulu War

4. Adverb + participle

a good-looking man	a well-nourished child

Comprehension

Comprehension is essentially the ability to understand a language. Understanding occurs at the levels of literal and implicit meaning. The reader then formulates an informed opinion about the topic. This assessment is arrived at by comparing what has been read with the accumulated knowledge and perception that the reader has previously acquired.

A comprehension test invites the candidate to apply, in writing, the skills used mentally each day. An effective way to practise these skills is to implement the following outline when reading closely.

1. PREPARE yourself by skimming over the passage. Look at the title, key words and phrases such as those starting or ending paragraphs; italicized or underlined words, anything else which catches your eye, such as the author's name. Take fifteen to twenty seconds per printed page.

2. QUESTION. Formulate questions based on what you remember from skimming the excerpt. These questions ought

to begin –
- What is meant by ...?
- What is the significance of ...?
- Who is ...?
- What is revealed about ...?
- Why is ...?
- How does the author ...?

3. READ the excerpt slowly, carefully and attentively.

4. SIFT through the questions you asked yourself – or those set in the comprehension exercise. Should there be any questions to which you do not yet know the answer, scan the excerpt for the relevant elements.

5. TELL: Talk to someone about what you've read. In an academic or business environment, 'telling' might involve writing down answers to set questions, compiling a report, or writing a summary.

6. In an academic reading assignment, do not waste words. Provide the answers in the format required – this may be a full sentence, a paragraph, a single word or phrase, a table, or a flow-chart. When you formulate your answers make sure that you are giving what is required: write a sentence if you are asked to do so, and explain if you are asked for a brief explanation.

Computer terms

Computers have acquired a vocabulary of their own. New words, acronyms and applications evolve so rapidly that regardless of experience users find themselves seeking definitions and explanations from their colleagues and in the trade publications. To complicate matters there are unique sets of vocabulary within various areas of computer activity. Mainframe specialists use words that are not used in relation to personal computers and vice versa.

Entire dictionaries of computer terms have been published to explain over 3000 words, acronyms and abbreviations. Included here are only a few of the most commonly encountered terms that often require explanation. (Note that the field of computers changes so rapidly that new terms are constantly being introduced to keep up with the technology. You may find that items in the list that follows have become outdated within a single year after publication.)

ASCII

Referred to by its acronym and pronounced "as-key", the American Standard Code for Information Interchange is a standard code that makes communication between various computers and computer programs possible. Files stored in ASCII format can, for example, be developed on one word processing program and retrieved and edited within another word processing program.

ATM

This abbreviation stands for Automatic Teller Machine. An ATM is a sophisticated terminal that enables a user to do banking operations by direct links to the bank's computer system, without any intervention by the staff of the bank.

AUTOEXEC.BAT

This is an abbreviation of Automatic Execute Batch File. When starting up a DOS-based personal computer, the autoexec.bat file executes automatically. By the inclusion of appropriate commands in this file, frequently used programs such as a word processing package load automatically. This file is usually referred to as the "autoexec" or the "autoexec dot bat" file.

Baud rates

A baud is one bit per second. The baud rate is the speed of data transmission, usually over a telephone line via a modem. The modem baud rates for personal computers fall between 300 and 28 800 (28.8 Kbps).

Bit

Bit is an acronym for binary digit. A bit is either a 0 or a 1. It is the smallest unit of information used on a computer.

Boot

'Booting up' is the term used to describe the starting up of a computer when you switch it on. It involves the implementation of the AUTOEXEC.BAT file and other files crucial to the operation of the computer.

Bug

A bug is an error in a computer program.

Byte

A byte is a group of eight bits. Computers recognize a byte as a single character or as a unit. The word is pronounced as 'bite'.

CAD/CAM

CAD is the acronym of computer-aided design. CAM is the acronym of Computer-aided Manufacturing. CAD essentially automates the function of the drafter in industrial design by using sophisticated software with the newest graphics capabilities. On the premise that computers can be used throughout the production process in a factory, from design to the end of manufacturing the product, CAD and CAM are used in combination.

Card

A card is a printed circuit board that consists of chips and wires. It is placed in a slot inside a personal computer to provide functions such as communications or graphics.

Chip

Usually made from silicon, a chip is an electronic component on which large amounts of information can be stored. Chips attached to a printed circuit board or motherboard form the basis of a computer. Chips can also perform functions such as arithmetic.

COMMAND.COM

This is a file used in DOS to store commands that make DOS function. It is usually referred to as the 'command-com file'.

CONFIG.SYS

The 'config-sys file', as it is usually called, is the DOS file that determines how the operating system will be set up on the computer.

Crash

A crash occurs when a serious programming error or a break in the power supply or the break-down of a hardware component results in the complete failure of a computer.

Debug

This means the correcting of errors in software.

Device driver

Word processing programs require the installation of a special computer software program, called a device driver, to run each device such as a printer or a mouse that is to be used.

DOS

This is an acronym for the Disk Operating System. It gets the computer running and controls the operation of what the computer does. DOS manages the flow, entry and display of both software and data to and from each component of the computer system. To run a software program, DOS has to be run first. While a program is being used, DOS moves instructions and files from one part of the computer system to another as commands are selected and information typed.

Double-Density Disk

This is a floppy disk which has twice the storage capacity of a single-density disk. Thus a 5,25 inch disk can hold 360K of data, and a double-density 3,5 inch disk can hold 720K.

Download

When data are transferred from a larger system, such as a

mainframe computer to a personal computer or workstation, this is called a download.

Dumb terminal

Computer terminals that have no processing capabilities, such as ones that are often attached to mainframe computers, are called dumb terminals.

E-mail

E-mail is an abbreviation of electronic mail. It describes communication through the sending and receiving of messages between two computers in the same building or in locations world-wide.

Encryption

Encryption is the translation of computer code into another code to prevent unauthorized access to the contents.

Fibre optics

This term describes a form of data transmission technology which uses glass or plastic threads inside insulated cabling to transmit data at the speed of light.

Floppy disk

Flexible diskettes, usually 5,25 inches or 3,5 inches in diameter, are called floppy disks. These disks are inserted in a floppy disk drive of a computer where data are stored on them or retrieved from them.

486

This abbreviation describes the Intel 80486 micro-processor or chip which is the key to the operation of many personal computers in use in the early to mid-1990s. It has largely been replaced by the pentium.

Hacker

Hackers are seriously interested computer users who learn largely by experimentation. They often do so by attempting to enter databases and computer systems without authorization.

Hackers may or may not seek to obtain information illegally or to cause damage to the data held in the system to which they have gained access.

Hard disk

Permanently installed inside the computer, the hard disk is a magnetic disk on which data are stored. Hard disks hold very much more data than do floppy disks and they are not as subject to damage.

Hardware

Hardware is the equipment comprising the central processing unit (or computer), cables, cords and devices such as printers and modems used for information storage and management.

High Density Disk

This floppy disk holds more data than a double-density disk. A 5,25 inch high-density disk holds 1,2 megabytes of data, and a 3,5 inch disk holds 1,44 megabytes.

Hypertext

This is an innovative database system in which a range of multimedia elements such as graphics, video, text and sound can be linked together.

Kilobyte

A kilobyte equals 1024 bytes.

LAN

The acronym of Local Area Network is LAN. It describes a system comprising personal computers in a department or office that are connected by cabling so as to share data and also application programs.

LCD

This is the abbreviation of Liquid Crystal Display. It describes a screen technology which uses light reflecting against a liquid crystal substance. These screens are often used in small portable computers and calculators.

Macro

A macro provides a quick way of writing a series of commands so as to execute functions that are used frequently. Using an application program's macro feature, the sequence of commands is entered and recorded before being given a macro name, often only one letter. Thereafter, when the macro name is entered, it causes the recorded sequence of commands to be repeated.

Mainframe

This is a large computer designed to handle the information needs of many users in a large institution. Mainframes are expensive and complicated to support. They are increasingly being augmented and even replaced by smaller computers and personal computers that are on local area networks.

Megabyte

One megabyte equals 1 048 576 bytes.

Megahertz

One million cycles per second in relation to electrical transmission is one megahertz. It is used to define the speed with which a personal computer operates.

Modem

A modem is a device for connecting a computer to a telephone line so that the computer can access online information in another computer or communicate with another computer.

Motherboard

The motherboard is the main circuit board of a microcomputer. It contains the central processing unit, ports and memory.

Mouse

A mouse is a device used to move the cursor around the screen. It is used to select required functions and issue commands. The mouse has two buttons that are clicked to make selections. The plural form is **mouses**.

Park

When a personal computer is to be transported, its disk drives are electronically locked or parked to avoid jarring and possible consequential damage. This is especially important with portable and laptop computers which are often moved.

PIN

This is the acronym of Personal Identification Number. It describes the code number or password unique to a specific user that prevents that user's file/s from being accessed by other users.

Program

A program is a list of instructions written in a computer language that cause a computer to process data and perform other specific operations. The American form of the word is in general use in South Africa in the context of computers. The word, when used in other contexts, is spelled **programme**.

RAM

RAM is the acronym of Random-access Memory. It describes the immediate or 'working' memory that can quickly be accessed in a computer, without requiring a search of storage areas. RAM holds the application program and associated data that are being used. It is not a permanent storage place and is active only when the computer is switched on.

ROM

ROM is the acronym of Read-only Memory. It describes the computer memory that contains the programs that are critical to the operation of the computer. When a computer is switched on, the instructions needed to boot the computer are drawn from the ROM.

Software

This is the term used to describe the set of programs and related documents that make a computer system perform functions.

Stiffy disk

This term is encountered in South Africa and is used incorrectly to describe the 3,5 inch floppy disk. The case protecting a 3,5 inch disk is rigid. The disk inside the casing is not.

VGA

This is the abbreviation of Video Graphics Array. It describes a video adapter that is standard for many personal computers and provides good graphics resolution. It is rapidly being superseded by Super VGA, which has a high-resolution graphics standard.

WAN

WAN describes a network of computers spread out over a large geographical area. It is the abbreviation of Wide-area Network.

Concave, convex

A **concave** surface is one which is curved like the inside of a ball. A **convex** surface is the opposite shape, curving like the outside of a ball.

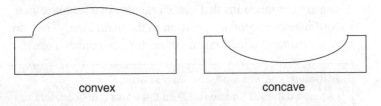

convex   concave

Conclusion

See: **Essay**

Concord

See: **Agreement**

Conjunctions

Conjunctions are words used to join words, phrases, or clauses. They are words like 'and', 'but', 'if', 'because', 'although', and 'and'.

There are two main types of conjunctions:

1. Coordinating conjunctions

These are conjunctions that join equal items.

> Khombe studies law, Fatima sells furniture, **and** Cathy writes novels.
>
> He will stay **or** I will leave.
>
> Mosa is not going, **nor** is her cousin staying.
>
> Kaiser Chiefs scored three goals, **but** they did not win the game.

Correlative conjunctions (such as 'both ... and', 'either ... or', and 'neither ... nor') are a special type of coordinating conjunction.

See: Both ... and; Correlative conjunctions; Whether, if

2. Subordinating conjunctions

These are conjunctions that place one idea in a sentence in a subordinate or secondary position to the main idea. (They are also sometimes called logical connectors, or connectives.)

> **Although** she was tired, she went to work.
>
> I accepted the job **because** I liked the working environment.
>
> **As** I didn't have cash on me, I paid by cheque.

Consonants

There are five vowels in the alphabet – a e i o u. The other twenty-one letters are known as consonants.

There are a few simple rules to remember about consonants:

1. **c** and **g** are pronounced softly before 'i' and 'e'.
   • Thus, when 'picnicking' is formed from 'picnic', the k is
   necessary to prevent the word from rhyming with 'dicing'.
   • When 'change' becomes 'changeable', 'e' must be retained
   (in an exception to the general rule) otherwise the **g** will not
   remain a soft sound.

2. When 'occur' becomes 'occurred' do not forget to double the
   consonant, **r**!

See: **Alliteration; Spelling; Vowels**

Context

1. Context refers to parts of a work appearing before and/or after
   a given statement, word or excerpt, with these parts affecting
   the meaning of the statement, word or excerpt.

> This quotation is from *Gulliver's Travels*, but I am not sure of its
> exact context.
>
> In the context of the Stock Exchange, it is correct to say that
> 'Gold is a volatile metal', but in the context of chemistry, you
> cannot describe gold as volatile!

2. Politicians sometimes claim that newspapers quote them 'out
   of context'. This means that phrases or words have been
   selectively quoted, giving a different meaning from that
   originally intended.

See: **Ellipsis**

Continual, continuity, continuous

1. **Continual** means 'going on all the time or with only short
   breaks'.

> Editing is a continual function of publishing.

85

2. **Continuous** refers to that which 'goes on without a break'.

> The continuous concentration required during every game during the World Chess Championship causes mental fatigue for the players.

3. **Continuity** refers to the 'state of being continuous'. A continuity announcer is a person on TV whose job it is to link the separate programmes into a continuous broadcast.

> An essay will not have continuity if you arrange your paragraphs in an illogical order, or if you leave out whole steps in your argument.

Contractions

1. A contraction is the shortened form of a word or a group of words. The missing letters are usually indicated by apostrophes. They are seldom acceptable in formal writing. They are often used in personal letters and notes, as well as in dialogue.

Contraction	Full form
can't	can not
don't	do not
isn't	is not
he'd	he would
shan't	shall not
she'll	she will
we're	we are
won't	will not
you've	you have

2. The mispronunciation of the contraction **could've** (could have) and **would've** (would have) has resulted in the meaningless combinations: 'could of', 'should of' and 'would of'.
3. Some contractions have become accepted practice, their origins having become obscure.

omnibus — bus	*bicycle* — bike (noun)
	cycle (verb)
of the clock — o'clock	*rhinoceros* — rhino
zoological gardens — zoo	*perambulator* — pram

See: **Abbreviations; Anomalous finite verbs; Its, it's**

Convex

See: **Concave**

Coordination

See: **Conjunctions**

Correction symbols

It is unlikely that there will ever be unanimity concerning a universal set of correction symbols for use by language teachers. The following list has proved pertinent, for the compilers, and entries are included in this book for each of them:

Symbol	Problem Area
Ab	Abbreviations
Agr	Agreement
Ap	Apostrophe
Cap	Capitals
CS	Comma splice

DM	Dangling modifier
Frag	Fragmentary sentence
L?	Logic
Org	Organization
P	Punctuation
Sp	Spelling
T	Tense
Wdy	Wordiness

Correlative conjunctions

Correlative conjunctions are pairs of conjunctions linking or 'correlating' two related items. Correlative conjunctions include the following:

both ... and	either ... or	neither ... nor
not only ... but also	rather ... than	whether ... or

See: Individual entries for each pair.

Criticize, criticism

This is the generic term for practical criticism, or critical analysis of a given text or excerpt. It implies the close, critical appraisal of such work, with any opinion or observation being supported by evidence from the text itself. When undertaking the critical appraisal of any given work –

1. Seek specific examples to support your argument
2. Check your assumptions
3. Quote from the text in support of your thesis
4. Check your conclusions, and ensure that you have not over-simplified, begged the question, or ignored the question.

See: **Instruction words**

88

Curriculum vitae (CV)

1. This is a brief account in writing of one's past history, including essential personal information, and it succinctly lists or summarizes one's education, qualifications and previous occupations. In South Africa it is usually called a CV. In the USA the word 'resumé' is used to describe this document.

2. Curriculum vitae is a Latin expression which means 'course of life' in direct translation. In English, the plural is curriculums vitae.

3. When one applies for a senior, professional, managerial or educational position, a requirement is often that one submits a copy of one's curriculum vitae. The contents are studied by the employer to decide whether the applicant's qualifications and experience seem appropriate for the vacant position. The impression created by one's curriculum vitae is therefore important and care should be taken to ensure that its contents are accurate, positive but without exaggeration or omission, and professionally presented.

4. One's CV should be carefully prepared for each different purpose and arranged to assist the reader. A CV submitted as part of a job application is of necessity more detailed than one used to assist the person introducing you when you have been asked to make a speech at some event. Bearing in mind the purpose for which the CV is being prepared, the following format will provide a useful starting point. Each section can be presented on a separate page so that copying and amendments can be more easily completed.

CURRICULUM VITAE

• **Personal details**
Full Name
Date of Birth and Identity Number
Marital Status
Names of spouse and children (with ages or dates of birth)
Residential address and home telephone number
Postal address (if this differs from the residential address)
Employer, business address and office telephone number
Private fax number and e-mail number (if appropriate)

Optional:
Language competence indicating reading, writing and speaking
fluency for each language
Religious affiliation
State of health
Interests and non-work related activities

• **Education**
Schooling indicating school/s and final examination results by subject
Tertiary education indicating institution/s, qualification/s and major
subjects
Other educational achievements, such as scholarships, bursaries,
fellowships, distinctions and prizes or awards
Membership of professional bodies where appropriate

• **Work experience**
List positions occupied throughout one's career, in descending order,
and mentioning specific duties
Periods of unemployment should be reflected

• **Publications/Research/Public Addresses**
Where appropriate - especially for an academic - these details will be
supplied

• **References**
Supply the names, addresses and telephone numbers of at least two

referees who are able to give confidential information on the applicant's personality, ability and work performance.This section is appropriate only in respect of applications. Referees should give their consent before they are listed, and in respect of every application.

• Present Salary
This is required by some employers and otherwise is optional.

Dangling modifier

1. Most dangling modifiers form the first part of a sentence, as in the following examples.

> X Filter or straight, men rate Gunston great!
>
> *It appears here as though men who like Gunston fall into two categories: those who are 'filter' (if there is such a creature), and those who are 'straight'! The sentence would be better phrased as follows.*
>
> √ Men rate Gunston great – whether filter or straight.

2. To correct the dangler, one needs to indicate directly after the phrase the person or object to whom or which the action relates.

See: **Participles**

Dare

See: **Anomalous finite verbs**

Dash (—)

A dash signifies a fairly long and dramatic pause. It is more commonly found in informal than in formal writing, as excessive use can give your writing a rather breathless and hysterical tone.

1. Dashes are used to add afterthoughts.

> We'll be entertaining the visiting American academics this weekend — that is, if they don't decide to go to the game reserve instead.

2. In informal writing, dashes can be used instead of colons or semi-colons.

> There are three things I cannot eat — lobster, prawns, and snails.

3. Dashes can be used to introduce or conclude an expression inserted into a sentence.

> The latest typewriters — so the advertisements claim — practically write your letters for you.

4. A dash is used at the end of an uncompleted sentence. (This is usually found in dialogue presented in fiction.)

> 'But darling —'
> 'Don't you 'darling' me!'

5. A dash starts off an afterthought or an aside. The afterthought or aside should always either be closed off with a second dash (as in the example under point 3 above) or with a full-stop (as in the other examples).

Data

1. The word 'data' is the plural of the Latin word 'datum' (meaning 'fact'). The word is thus plural and should take a plural verb and plural pronouns.

> What are the data in this case?
> The data have been collated. They present some interesting anomalies.

2. In American usage, 'data' is seen as a singular, collective noun, and the word is used with a singular verb and singular pronouns. South African usage increasingly follows the American.

Dates

1. For years the logical order used was that of day, month, year: 6 July 1999. However, people also use 6th July 1999 or July 6th, 1999 or July 6, 1999. The lack of standardization can cause confusion when only figures are used.

2. In an endeavour to eradicate ambiguity, officialdom decreed that, in South Africa, we would follow the international dating system and use year, month, day: 1999-07-06. Of course confusion continues, for elsewhere in the world the practice which prevails is year, day, month!

3. The names of months which cannot be abbreviated are May, June and July. The others can be shortened as follows: Jan, Feb, Mar, Apr, Aug, Sept, Oct, Nov, Dec.

4. Spell out 'twentieth century' for the period from 1901 to 2000. The first year of the twenty-first century will be 2001.

See: **Apostrophe; Numbers**

Definite, definitely

1. The adjective **definite** means to be 'clear, certain, precise and not vague'.

> There is a definite change in the weather.

2. The definite article is 'the'.

See: **Articles; Determiners; The**

3. The adverb, **definitely**, means 'in a definite manner'.
However, it also has a colloquial meaning of 'yes, certainly'
when it is used in answer to a question.

> You will definitely find a hotel in that vicinity.
> Colloquial example:
> 'Are you going to the "fliek" tonight?'
> 'Definitely.'

Definite article

The is the definite article.

See: **Articles; Determiners; The**

Delusion

See: **Allusion**

Demonstratives

1. Demonstrative pronouns indicate persons or things:

this   that   those   these   such

2. Take care to ensure that the person or thing to which a
demonstrative pronoun refers is clearly indicated.

> *The following is somewhat confusing:*
>
> X The first step in planting wheat is to turn over the soil.
> This should be done to a depth of 15 cm.
> In early days this was done by means of a plough pulled by oxen.
> Nowadays tractors do this.
>
> *The following is acceptable:*
>
> √ Many farmers have only a few days to prepare the soil before planting.
> This should be taken into consideration when the activities for the year are planned.

See: **Ambiguity; Pronouns**

Dependant, dependent

1. **Dependant** is a noun and is used for an individual who depends on another.

> In addition to his own family, he provides for two other dependants, his mother and his great-aunt.

2. The adjective **dependent** has two meanings.

   • The first is similar to that of the noun.

> In addition to his own family, he provides for two other dependent relatives.

   • The second meaning defines one thing as being subject to another.

> Her permanent appointment was dependent upon the quality of her performance in her initial year of probation.

96

Derivations

1. One word can be derived from another word by adding a **derivational affix**. An affix can be added to the beginning of a word (it is then called a prefix) or the end of a word (a suffix). See the entries on prefixes and suffixes for a detailed discussion of these.

2. See also the entries on adjectives and adverbs for the derivation of these words from other words.

Description

1. Here are four steps of description outlined in the 1983 edition of Sheridan Baker's *The Practical Stylist* (New York: Harper & Row):

   • What is it NOT like?
   • What is it like?
   • What is it not?
   • What is it?

2. Other avenues to follow include:

   • Description by function: what something or someone does.
   • Description by synthesis: placing the subject of the description in a relationship with similar items.
   • Description by example: the giving of examples and illustrations in order to broaden the description.
   • Description by comparison: describing by comparing the subject with something different (or, perhaps, fairly similar).

See also **Essays; Instruction words; Paragraphs**

Determiners

1. Determiners are words which 'determine' nouns or noun

phrases. There are two groups of determiners.

Group 1 Determiners

Articles:	a	an	the
Possessive pronouns:	my		your
	his		hers
	its		theirs
	one's		whose
Demonstrative pronouns:	this	that	these	those

Group 2 Determiners

some	any	no	each
every	either	neither	much
many	more	most	little
less	least	few	fewer
fewest	enough	several	all
both	half		

2. If a Group 2 determiner is placed before a Group 1 determiner, 'of' must be inserted.

> some of the children
> many of these books
> all of my clothes

3. Two determiners from one group cannot be used together.

> X the my house
> X some many people

Development of paragraphs

See: **Paragraphs**

Dewey classification

The Dewey classification is the system used by our libraries
for the arrangement of books. There are ten main sections,
each of which is divided into ten parts. In turn each of these
sub-sections is divided up, and so on until every class of book
is categorized and allotted its place on the library shelves.

The ten main sections are –

000 General
100 Philosophy
200 Religion
300 Social Science
400 Languages
500 Science
600 Useful Arts
700 Fine Arts
800 Literature
900 Geography
    Biography
    History

The books are arranged on the shelves according to the
numerical category into which they are placed under the
Dewey Classification system. Within each numerical
classification the books are then arranged in the alphabetical
order of the authors' surnames.

Dialect

Different regions within a country sometimes have different
dialects, or forms of the language spoken in the country.
Tsotsitaal or *flaai* are examples of dialect. Teenagers often
have a dialect of their own characterized by a specific
vocabulary and rules of interaction. One should always,
however, use standard formal language in writing, unless

reporting dialect in direct speech.

Dialogue

1. Dialogue has become a vogue-word. It is used to describe an exchange of views between leaders.

> A dialogue between the Presidents of the two states was initiated.

2. The more conventional meaning of dialogue is 'writing in the form of conversation or talk'. Essentially, **direct speech** is recorded in such a way that the reader can discover exactly what was said and by whom. Inverted commas are used to differentiate between the dialogue itself and the accompanying explanations.

> 'Oh no,' said Coleridge, 'nothing of that kind, but it is something that I cannot think of without the deepest pain.'
>
> 'Well,' said Rose, 'let us hear it: perhaps it is not so bad as you at this moment consider it.'
>
> 'I came to you', added Coleridge, 'as a friend and a clergyman, to ask you what I ought under the circumstances to do.'
>
> 'Let me have the circumstances', rejoined Rose, 'and then I may be better able to judge. Calm yourself!'
>
> From J P Collier's *An Old Man's Diary, Forty Years Ago*

3. In the writing of dialogue an author may deliberately cause some of his characters to speak imperfect English. This adds to the authenticity of their speech as conversation contains many errors and inconsistencies.

4. Take note of the punctuation in the given example:

- Inverted commas are used.
- There is a comma after 'Oh no' and 'Well', as well as all the other interspersed statements.
- The exclamation mark is used where it is appropriate.
- Each new speaker's comments begin with a new paragraph.

See: **Direct speech; Quotation marks**

Dictionary

1. A dictionary is a book containing the words of a language – with the words arranged alphabetically. When in doubt, consult a dictionary, nearly all of which have a preface explaining the arrangements of entries, and a key to the pronunciation(s) of words.

2. Dictionary entries give you the following information:

- spelling
- pronunciation
- part of speech
- meaning
- Some dictionaries also provide the derivation of a word.

Die / dye

1. To **die** is to pass away, to lose life.

2. To **dye** is to change the colour of something.

3. Confusion in spelling can cause considerable confusion in a reader's mind, so care should be taken in spelling the various forms of the two words.

Human beings are the only creatures who know that they will die.

Dying is a painful and lonely experience.

When he died, the whole nation mourned.

In the long run, we are all dead.

Does she dye her hair?

Dying one's hair blond can change one's entire image.

Dyed hair always betrays itself by its roots.

Different from

1. 'Different from' versus 'different to' has been a hotly debated contest in many linguistic circles. Both expressions are, ultimately, acceptable, although each expression has vociferous critics. American usage favours 'different than'. This expression is not acceptable in South African English.

2. 'Differ from' (as in 'My political views differ from yours') is, however, the only correct form of the verb phrase. The expression 'differ to' is incorrect.

Direct speech

1. Direct speech is used when we report the exact words used by a person. Cartoons use direct speech in the speech 'bubbles' for each character:

Reproduced by courtesy of Rapid Phase

102

2. Direct speech can also be written in the form of a dialogue (as in plays). The dialogue form of the cartoon would be written as follows:

> MADAM: Okay, Eve – Let's rehearse! ... And here's your question: What would you *do* if you became Miss South Africa?
> EVE: I would do my best to bring about world peace, help underprivileged people, little animals ... and protect the environment.
> MADAM: What do you think?
> MOM: Vacuous, meaningless and without any *substance* whatsoever!
> MOM & MADAM: Perfect!!
>
> (Note that each character's name is followed by a colon, and that no quotation marks are used.)

3. In narrative writing, direct speech is incorporated into the text as follows. (Note that each character's contribution is given a new paragraph.)

> 'Who are you talking to?' said the King, coming up to Alice and looking at the Cat's head with great curiosity.
>
> 'It's a friend of mine – A Cheshire Cat –' said Alice, 'allow me to introduce it.'
>
> 'I'd rather not,' the Cat remarked.
>
> *Alice in Wonderland* by Lewis Carroll

See: **Dialogue; Quotation marks**

4. When the speaker's exact words are not given, we use Indirect or Reported Speech. In indirect speech, the Madam and Eve dialogue would be written as follows:

Madam suggested to Eve that they should rehearse. She asked Eve what she would do if she became Miss South Africa. Eve answered that she would do her best to bring about world peace, help underprivileged people, little animals and protect the environment. Madam then asked Mom what she thought. Mom labelled Eve's answer vacuous, meaningless and without any substance whatsoever. Then they both exclaimed that the response was perfect.

See: **Indirect speech**

Disinterested, uninterested

1. A person who is **disinterested** is impartial or without self interest.

He was disinterested in the outcome of the rugby game, but drew pleasure from noting the skill with which the players handled the muddy ball.

2. An **uninterested** person, on the other hand, is one without interest or enthusiasm.

The uninterested woman who sat next to me at the cricket yesterday only paused in her humming and knitting long enough to punctuate every dramatic moment in the game with an inane question about what had just happened.

Division of words into syllables

See: **Hyphen**

Do

See: **Anomalous finite verbs**

Doctor

1. Note that this word is spelt with two o's.

2. The abbreviation of the title is **Dr** without a full-stop and is used only in combination with the name of the individual.

> What should I do, Dr Moosa?
>
> What should I do, Doctor?
>
> Has your doctor been to see you yet?

3. As an abbreviation, Dr is always written with a capital letter.

4. In direct speech, where the doctor is addressed, a capital D is used. Any general reference to doctors is not capitalized.

Double comparison

Words like 'inferior' and 'superior' inherently have the features of a comparative adjective. As such they cannot be used in conjunction with the word 'more'.

See: **Adjectives**

Double negative

See: **Negative**

Drama

Drama refers to the literary genre of works (including plays) intended to be performed on the stage. Shakespeare's plays fall within this genre.

Due to, owing to

These are commonly confused, but the distinction is as follows:

1. **Owing to** is a compound preposition introducing an adverb phrase.

> Owing to the bad weather, we were delayed.

2. **Due to** is used for adjectival constructions.

> The delay was due to bad weather.

3. A simple way to remember the distinction is to note that **owing to** generally means 'because of', while **due to** means 'caused by'.

Each

1. **Each** can act as an adjective or a pronoun, and means 'every one taken separately'.

> Each new day offers new opportunities.

2. **Each** always takes a singular verb.

> Each one of us is determined to do the best we can.

3. **Each** implies that we are thinking of the members of a group separately, while 'every' implies that we are thinking of all the members of the group together. ('Every' is thus closer in meaning to 'all'.)

> I want each student in my class to feel respected as an individual.
> I would like every student at the university to take full advantage of the educational opportunities offered.

See: **Determiners; Everybody, everyone, every**

-ed, -t

1. In the case of certain words **-t** replaces the **-ed** ending. The usage is not governed by pronunciation.

> burnt   dreamt   knelt   spelt   spilt

107

2. The **-ed** ending is archaic, and more formal. It usually occurs as a past tense form, or is used with 'have'.

See: **Participles; -t, -ed; Verbs**

Effect / effective

See: **Affect, effect; Affective, effective**

eg

See: **ie; viz**

Either ... or

1. **Either ... or** are correlative conjunctions. That is, they join a pair of related items.

2. **Either** is used with **or** to juxtapose two possibilities.

> Either you resign, or we'll fire you.
> You can either send us a cheque later, or pay in cash now.

3. It is important that the structures be balanced, and that the same kind of structure follows **either** and **or**.

> I should like to work either in Cape Town or in Durban.
>
> NOT   X I should like either to work in Cape Town or in Durban

4. Appropriate forms of the verb should be used to agree with each item.

> Either she is or I am likely to be the next managing director

Elder, older

1. The words **elder** and **eldest** are confined to use in the context of family relationships.

2. **Older** and **oldest** are used as the comparative and superlative forms in other contexts.

> My elder sister is starting university this year, and next year will be my turn.
>
> Temba is the eldest of the three brothers.
>
> Faizel is the oldest boy in his class.
>
> This car is older than that one.

Ellipsis (...)

1. **Ellipsis** means the device whereby words are omitted from a sentence. Three dots (called **ellipses**) marked off with a space at either end (...) are used to indicate that words have been left out of a quotation.

Mr Chris Heunis, addressing an American audience, stated that the government planned 'to restructure the historically determined hierarchical system of apartheid into something based on the premise of divided power and joint structures in which discrimination – and this goes without saying – will have to go, but without jeopardizing the non-negotiables of the maintenance of group interests and aspirations within the wider context of security and stability.'

This quotation can be shortened, using ellipsis, as follows:

Mr Chris Heunis stated that the government planned 'to restructure the ... system of apartheid into something based on the premise of divided power and joint structures in which discrimination ... will have to go ... without jeopardizing the non-negotiables of the maintenance of group interests and aspirations ...'.

2. Note that a full-stop follows the ellipses at the end of a sentence.

3. It is, needless to say, unethical to use ellipsis to distort the meaning of the original text, as in the following example.

X Mr Chris Heunis stated that the government planned 'to restructure the ... system of apartheid into something based on the premise of ... discrimination ... without ... the maintenance of group interests and aspirations ...'.

Elude

See: **Allude**

Embarrass

If you embarrass others, you disconcert them or cause them anxiety. The word is spelt with two A's, R's and S's.

Emigrate, immigrate

1. To **emigrate** is to leave one country and to settle in another.

> He emigrated from South Africa to Australia.

2. To **immigrate** is to come to a country (in which one was not born) in order to settle there permanently.

> The family in the house on the corner has immigrated from Zaire.

3. A simple rule of thumb is to remember the following equations:

| to go away from a country | = | to emigrate |
| to come into a country | = | to immigrate |

Emotive language

See: **Feeling in words**

Endorse

This word has three meanings.

1. **Endorse** can mean the writing of one's signature on the back of a cheque.

> She endorsed the cheque.

2. It may also mean writing comments on a document.

> His arrest for drunken driving led to his driving licence being endorsed.

3. Thirdly, it may mean an expression of approval.

> He endorsed all of her comments with enthusiasm.

Enjambement (enjambment)

1. Enjambement is a device used in poetry.

> Sweetest love, I do not go
> For weariness of thee ...
>
> John Donne

2. Notice that at the close of the first line, you move with

111

virtually no pause to the next line. Such lines are called run-on, and the effect of continuity they provide is referred to as enjambement or enjambment.

3. When the lines close on a strong pause we call them **end-stopped**.

> My Daphne's hair is twisted gold,
> Bright stars apiece her eyes do hold ...
>
> John Lyly

Envelopes

See: **Addressing envelopes**

Epic

The term **Epic** is applied to a work that is -

- on a major and serious subject;
- presented in an elevated style; and
- focused on a heroic figure on whose actions depends the fate of a people, or a nation, or the human race.

-er, -or

1. The usual rule for converting a word from a verb into a noun, which describes the doer of the action, is to add **-er** or **-r** where the verb ends in '-e'. The following words end in -er and should be remembered:

builder	feeder	kicker	plumber
adviser	computer	promoter	propeller
conjurer *(although conjuror has gained acceptance)*			

2. These words are often mis-spelt because of confusion caused
   by words, especially those derived from Latin, which end in
   -or.

actor	collector	conqueror	distributor
tailor	ejector	error	governor
impostor	sailor		

See: **Spelling**

Erotica

Erotica is a plural noun and is used to describe books, theatre,
magazines and pictures that are intended to arouse sexual
excitement or desire. Such material seeks to stimulate feelings
that are erotic rather than aesthetic or emotional. When the
subject matter of erotica is obscene, especially reflecting
sexual perversions, it is described as pornographic.

See: **Pornography**

Errors, common

There are separate entries for each of these common errors,
but they are summarized here.

1. Abbreviations
   In formal writing avoid the use of abbreviations and
   contractions. Rather than use the perennial favourite of
   students, 'etc', try to rephrase the statements.

See: **Abbreviations; Contractions**

2. Agreement

X Each of the girls have a pretty dress to wear.

√ Each of the girls has a pretty dress to wear.
The verb is 'has' because the subject 'each' is singular.

See: **Agreement**

113

3. Apostrophe

Many writers insert apostrophes in plural nouns and sometimes in singular verbs.

> X marble's, potato's, rock's, kick's, slide's.
> √ marbles, potatoes, rocks, kicks, slides.

Another problem in South Africa is a growing tendency to duplicate possession.

> X That book of John's needs a new cover.
> *(You should not use the possessive 'of' together with the possessive apostrophe.)*
>
> √ John's book needs a new cover.

See: **Apostrophe**

4. Audience

Writers must always keep their audience or readers in mind. A prevalent error is to alter the audience inadvertently in the middle of a piece of prose writing.

See: **Audience, reader**

5. Capitals

Afrikaans influences some writing.

> X a Tree is a thing of value.
> √ A tree is a thing of value.

Other areas of difficulty are caused by ignorance of the rules of capitalization.

See: **Capitals**

6. Case of pronoun

X They would rather play with Zuzu and I.

√ They would rather play with Zuzu and me.

Prepositions are usually followed by the objective case, which requires 'me' not 'I'.

See: **Case; You and I**

Another pronoun problem frequently encountered in South Africa is the use of unrelated pronouns.

X The weather changed overnight and a storm blew up. It is not surprising.

There is confusion here over whether the pronoun refers to the weather or the storm or the change.

See: **Ambiguity; Clumsy expression**

7. Dangling modifiers

Do not allow an introductory or concluding part of a sentence to dangle without a word or group of words to modify.

X Having seen the menu, my order was given immediately.

Obviously the order could not have seen the menu. Rephrase the sentence.

√ Having seen the menu, I gave my order immediately.

See: **Dangling modifier**

8. Comma splice

Do not use a comma to separate two independent clauses or sentences that are not joined by a coordinating conjunction.

X Stringing the wires to the fuse box is not too hard, making the final connections is even easier.

RATHER

√ Stringing the wires to the fuse box is not too hard; making the final connections is even easier.

X Building regulations vary from one city to the next, therefore, a wise person will check them before beginning.

RATHER

√ Building regulations vary from one city to the next. Therefore, a wise person will check them before beginning.

See: **Comma; Comma splice**

9. Fragmentary sentence

The chief problem in this context is that there is often no verb. Hence what has been written is a non-sentence.

X Our heating costs remained the same. Instead of going down.

√ Our heating costs remained the same instead of going down.

See: **Fragmentary sentence**

10. Idiom

Errors of idiom are eliminated only by copious practice in reading, speaking and writing the language.

X Campbell has been acclaimed by many of being South Africa's greatest poet.

√ Campbell has been acclaimed by many to be South Africa's greatest poet.

See: **Idioms**

11. Logic

Avoid sweeping generalizations or leaping to conclusions; strive for logical thinking.

> X All South African students today are again giving serious attention to their studies and avoiding political activism.
>
> *As there are surely some South African students who are not giving their studies close attention, and as there are certainly some who are political activists, this statement's logic is faulty. Omitting 'all' still makes this statement a sweeping generalization. Phrasing the opening of the sentence in order not to overstate the case will rectify the statement.*
>
> √ Many South African students today are again giving serious attention to their studies and avoiding political activism.

See: **Logic**

12. Organization

The reader responds best to a controlled, structured development of a theme. There are many forms of organization open to the writer: sequential, chronological, increasing-order-of-importance, decreasing-order-of-importance, division and classification, comparison, spatial, specific-to-general, general-to-specific and cause-and-effect. Once your method of development is fixed, compose an outline. Give attention to the beginning, middle and end of your writing.

See: **Organization; Instruction words**

13. Punctuation

The worst punctuation errors are the misuse of the apostrophe and the excessive use of the comma, especially in the form of a comma splice.

See: **Comma; Comma splice; Punctuation**

117

14. Sentences
   • Use uncomplicated sentences to state complex ideas. Do not inconsistently shift structure in the middle of a sentence.

   > X A bursary enabled me to continue my education and not finding a job right away.
   >
   > √ A bursary enabled me to continue my education and to postpone finding a job right away.

   • Ensure that the subject and the rest of the sentence are compatible.

   > X Because my alarm clock did not go off is why I was late.
   >
   > √ I was late because my alarm clock did not go off.

   • Ensure that the constituents in any series in a sentence are parallel in structure.

15. Avoid dangling modifiers
   Place modifiers in sentences so that the modified word or group of words is immediately clear.

   > X If the milk does not agree with the baby, boil it.
   > √ Boil the milk if it does not agree with the baby.
   >
   > X After conducting a long search, a used car was bought by my daughter whose body was in good shape.
   > √ After conducting a long search, my daughter bought a used car whose body was in good shape.

   See: **Modifiers; Sentences**

16. Slang
   In formal writing avoid slang and colloquialisms, except in the reproduction of direct speech.

   See: **Colloquialisms; Slang**

17. Spelling

Many spelling errors can be corrected by carefully reading over what has been written.

See: **Spelling**

18. Tense

The verb of a subordinate clause should usually agree in tense with the main verb.

Avoid illogical shifts in tense as these confuse the reader.

> X When Ms Ngengebule **dictated** a letter, she **wants** it typed immediately.
>
> √ When Ms Ngengebule **dictates** a letter, she **wants** it typed immediately.
>
> √ When Ms Ngengebule **dictated** a letter, she **wanted** it typed immediately.

See: **Agreement; Tenses; Verbs**

19. Wordiness

Write concisely and precisely. Do not ramble or use excess words. Decide what you mean; then set it down clearly.

> X I like the biographical information about Austen's life better than her fictitious novels.
> *(If it is 'biographical information', it is about 'Austen's life'; novels are 'fictitious'.)*
>
> √ I like Austen's biography better than her novels.

See: **Wordiness**

Essay, planning

1. An essay is a piece of extended writing consisting of more than one paragraph, and has a beginning, middle and end. The following is a useful outline:

119

- Introductory paragraph (about 75 words)
- Middle paragraphs (100–150 words for each paragraph)
- Concluding paragraph (as for the first paragraph)

2. Your essay also needs to have a thesis statement, which introduces the theme of the essay in the first paragraph. The middle paragraphs each develop a single major idea which is linked to the thesis statement. The major idea in these paragraphs is in each case indicated by a single topic sentence. The ideas suggested for the organization of paragraphs can thus be extended and applied to the organization and planning of an essay.

- Paragraph 1
Introduction, containing thesis statement of the essay
- Paragraph 2
Middle paragraph, containing a topic sentence and supporting argument
- Paragraph 3
Middle paragraph, containing a topic sentence and supporting argument
- Paragraph 4
Middle paragraph, containing a topic sentence and supporting argument
- Paragraph 5
Conclusion, drawing the threads of the essay together, and showing how the thesis statement has been developed.

See: **Description; Instruction words; Paragraphs; Revision**

Essay, writing

The writing of an essay is the culmination of a number of processes: research, understanding of sentence construction, awareness of paragraph construction and planning.

Here, in brief, are some hints concerning research and a few things to bear in mind when writing the first draft of an essay.

1. Research

   Once you have studied the essay question, and have planned the work in broad detail, assemble the data (the results of your reading) on separate index cards, with only one fact or idea on each card. Record the sources of your quotations on the applicable cards, as this is much easier than having to search for the information once the first draft is complete. Then sort the cards according to your essay plan. You are now ready to write the first draft.

   See: **Referencing**

2. Hints when writing the first draft
   • Select details carefully: choose information that is interesting and important.
   • Avoid wordiness by using precise, vivid verbs, and by using adjectives only when necessary.
   • Make your writing specific and concrete.

   'Hamlet seems on the verge of insanity'
   is generalized and vague, whereas
   'The way in which Hamlet confronts Ophelia indicates someone who has difficulty coming to terms with what he perceives to be reality' *is more specific.*

   • Ensure that there is a proper order to the presentation of ideas: an essay is not merely a mass of information and ideas thrown together, but should progress systematically from a starting point (the thesis statement) to a concluding paragraph (which contains some indication as to how you believe you have proved or addressed the thesis statement).
   • If possible, set the first draft aside for a day or two, which will allow you to approach revision with a fresh eye and enable you to see errors you might otherwise overlook. Revise the first draft carefully, and then rewrite it. (Many of us skip this stage in the mistaken belief that it is unnecessary: the results are often disastrous!)

   See: **Instruction words; Proofreading; Revision**

Etc

1. Etc is an abbreviation of the Latin 'et cetera', meaning 'and the rest', or 'and so forth'.

2. The use of this abbreviation all too often indicates a lazy and nonchalant approach to one's subject matter. Etc should be used only when the style of writing justifies it and where space is at a premium. In formal writing, and in writing where the aim is effective and complete communication, its use should be avoided.

See: **Abbreviations**

Euphemism

This is the opposite of blunt directness. It occurs when we ask 'When did your father pass away?' rather than 'When did your father die?' Use euphemism carefully (if at all) in formal writing.

See: **Abstractions; Feeling in words; Wordiness**

Everybody, everyone, every

1. **Everybody** and **everyone** are pronouns referring to all the individuals who make up a group. These pronouns are singular, and – in formal writing – pronouns, possessives and verbs related to them should also be singular.

> Everyone seems to have his own opinion on the subject.
> Everybody was delighted by the raise in salary.

2. **Every** refers to the single members of a group.

> Every dog has his day.
> Every one of these typewriters has been serviced.

122

3. Writers who want to avoid sexist bias in their writing have the option of the clumsy 's/he' and 'his/her' construction, or of exclusively using 'she' and 'her' (which replaces one sexist bias with another), or of using the plural pronouns 'they' and 'their' to refer back to 'everyone' and 'everybody'. This use is frowned upon by prescriptive grammarians, but has nevertheless been colloquially acceptable for over a hundred years.

See: **Agreement; Anybody, anyone; Sexist language**

Exaggeration

Exaggeration, like hyperbole, can be used to lend emphasis to what we are saying or writing. It should, however, be used sparingly and judiciously. For example, we might say to a friend that 'One has to wait for several centuries in that doctor's rooms' or 'Our new teacher dates from the dinosaurs', and this would be acceptable – even though colloquial. In formal writing, however, exaggeration tends to make one sound subjective, inaccurate, unacademic, and unprofessional. The sentences thus would be better rephrased as: 'One has to wait some time to see that particular doctor'; 'Our new teacher is fairly old'.

See: **Understatement**

Except

1. **Except** is a preposition and is followed by the object form of the pronoun (me, him, her, them).

> Everybody seems to have heard about the reasons for his dismissal, except me.

2. **Except** should not be confused with **accept**, which means to consent to something, or to regard with favour.

123

> I accepted his apology.

See: **Accept, except**

Excerpt

This is generally a short piece or passage taken from a longer work for detailed criticism or examination on its own. You are usually expected to relate the excerpt to the context of the longer work.

> Critically examine the following excerpt from *Waiting for the Barbarians*.
> Choose several excerpts from the novel in support of your argument.

Exclamation mark (!)

1. As its name implies, the exclamation mark is used primarily after exclamations.

> Look out!
> Help!

2. Exclamation marks are also used to express sarcasm.

> Oh, you clever ass!

3. Exclamation marks should be avoided in formal writing, as they tend to evoke mistrust and irritation in your reader because of the melodramatic tone they create.

4. Multiple exclamation marks, as in 'Here's my report at last!!!' are both unprofessional and extremely irritating to your reader.

Explicit, implicit

1. The adjective, **explicit**, means 'clearly, fully and directly stated'.

2. **Implicit** is also an adjective and it usually means 'suggested, but not plainly expressed'; the alternative meaning of implicit is 'unquestioning'.

> The terms of his employment are explicit: he is entitled to sick leave only after he has worked there for six months.
>
> The implicit meaning behind her response can only be derived by reading between the lines.
>
> We have implicit faith in your leadership.

See: **Imply, infer**

Fabulous

1. **Fabulous** means that which is mythical or celebrated in legends and fables. A second meaning of this adjective is 'incredible'.

> The fabulous tales contained in Aesop's Fables have captivated and educated readers for years.
> The fabulous wealth of the Shah was evident in the palace he built.

2. In recent times the word has acquired an illogical, but extensively used, colloquial meaning of 'wonderful or marvellous'. This use is out of place in formal writing.

> X It was one of those fabulous all-night parties.

See: **Misused words**

Fantastic

1. **Fantastic**, an adjective, has two major meanings: that which is 'wild, strange and grotesque', or that which is 'absurd or impossible to do'.

> After a night of fantastic dreams Coleridge awoke and dashed off the first lines of 'Kubla Khan'.
>
> He outlined his fantastic plan for kidnapping the President to his accomplices.

126

2. Recently the word has acquired the slang meaning 'wonderful or marvellous'.

> X They are fantastic company.

See: **Misused words**

Farther, further

These words are fast becoming interchangeable, meaning 'to a great distance or degree'. In formal usage **farther** and **farthest** are preferred when used in terms of physical distance.

> Kakamas is the farthest town from here.
> He spoke further on the subject.

Faulty parallelism

See: **Parallel structures**

Feeling in words

1. Words have both denotations and connotations. The **denotations** of a word are its objective meanings – the meanings you will find when you look up that word in a dictionary. The connotations of a word are the associations, feelings, sensations, opinions and ideas that the word evokes.

2. Words can have negative connotations, positive connotations, or neutral connotations. By one's choice of words with specific **connotations**, one can describe the same thing in different ways. For example, if you have a friend who is worried about her weight, you may try to reassure her by describing her as 'plump' or 'curvaceous' – words with positive connotations. Her doctor might describe her as

'overweight' – a fairly neutral term. Someone who didn't like your friend or who wanted to hurt her feelings would possibly describe her as 'fat' – a word which, in Western culture, has negative connotations.

The table below gives you examples of words with positive, negative, and neutral connotations:

Negative	Neutral	Positive
fat	overweight	plump, curvaceous
skinny	underweight	slim, slender, willowy
crafty	intelligent	bright, brilliant
miserly	careful with money	frugal
flirtatious	friendly	charming
obstinate	determined	resolute
terrorist	—	freedom fighter
mob	crowd, group	gathering

3. Politicians and advertisers are known for using emotive language – language which depends heavily on the connotations of its vocabulary. Any text aimed at influencing the reader's or listener's opinions will rely on the connotations of words to affect the audience's feelings. This kind of text often uses what are called 'loaded words', words which carry an unusually heavy weight of connotations. Writers try to arouse reactions in their audience by using words loaded with positive connotations (such as 'patriotism', 'freedom', or 'democracy'), or words that are loaded with negative connotations (such as 'racism', 'discrimination' or 'oppression').

See: **Synonyms**

Fewer, less

1. A general rule is that one uses **fewer** for numbers, and **less** for amounts.

fewer spectators	less food
fewer letters	less money

2. **Fewer** is the comparative of 'few', while **less** is the comparative of 'little'.

> I have a few friends, but Anne has even fewer.
> Dogs have little intelligence, but cats seem to have less.

3. Without the article ('a'), **few** tends to have a negative meaning.

> I have few friends.
> *This sentence implies that one does not have as many friends as one would like.*
>
> I have a few friends.
> *Here the meaning is a little more positive. 'A few' tends to suggest 'more than one would expect'.*

Figurative language

1. This is a device which occurs in many different forms of creative writing. It is a means of indirect statement that says one thing in terms of another and, if well used, brings the reader very close to the essence of an idea while conveying a sense of the writer's feelings or attitude.

> Time held me green and dying
> Though I sang in my chains like the sea.
>
> Dylan Thomas: 'Fern Hill'

2. In their own work, beginning writers should be wary of

figurative language as it can seem foolish if it is not used appropriately.

Figures of speech

1. A **figure of speech** is an unusual or striking use of words. This unusual use is designed for a specific effect or emphasis.

2. The following figures of speech have individual entries in this handbook:

   Alliteration
   Assonance
   Exaggeration / Hyperbole
   Metaphor
   Simile
   Understatement

Finite and non-finite verbs

1. A **finite verb** is one that is complete, that has tense and number. The main verb of a sentence must always be a finite verb.

   > He is running.
   > Despite being ill, he chaired the meeting.
   > I may be late tomorrow.

2. A **non-finite verb** is one that is not complete in itself.

   > ... hoping to hear from you soon ...
   > ... singing in the chapel ...
   > ... written to you last week ...
   > ... stolen from me at work ...

3. A **non-finite verb** cannot be the main verb of a sentence.

Flee, fly

1. **To flee** is to run away from, or to escape from.

> Donald Woods fled the country. In fleeing, he crossed the border secretly.

2. **To fly** is to move through the air by means of wings (natural or mechanical).

> I enjoy flying and last year flew to Cape Town several times rather than drive. Having flown to a destination does mean, however, that one has to arrange for transport once there.

Footnotes

1. A **footnote** provides your reader with precise identification of the source of a quotation, or supplies further information on a particular point.

2. You should provide a footnote whenever you –
   • use a direct quotation
   • copy a table, chart, or diagram
   • summarize a discussion in your own words
   • construct a diagram from data provided by others
   • wish to provide additional detail on a specific point

3. There are two parts to a footnote: the number that appears in the text of your paper; and the actual reference, which may be placed at the bottom of the page on which the number occurs, or in a list at the end of the paper, section, or chapter.

4. Rules
   • Footnotes are numbered consecutively throughout your paper, or chapter.

- Footnote numbers in the text come after the information cited, or the quotation, and usually after all the punctuation in your sentence.
- No parentheses or other punctuation should be used around the footnote number.
- The footnote itself is separated from the text by a triple space or short ruled line.
- The author's name is given in its normal order – first name(s) and surname.
- The title is given only in the first reference. In subsequent references only the author's surname is necessary, unless more than one work by the same author is being used.
- Place, publisher, and date of publication are given only in the first reference, and thereafter omitted.

See: **Plagiarism; Referencing**

Foreign words

1. When a foreign word will capture your meaning more accurately or appropriately than an English one, use it in *italics*, provided that the reader will understand the expression. The overuse of foreign words is irritating and, given the richness of English, unwarranted.

2. Many foreign words, such as 'milieu', 'crisis' or 'index', have been absorbed by English and do not need to be italicized.

> She graduated *cum laude*, having obtained distinctions in all of her subjects.
>
> The demonstrators *toyi-toyied* without a break throughout the day as the number in their ranks grew.
>
> Increasing numbers of black South Africans are joining the ranks of the *bourgeoisie* as employment opportunities open up for them.

3. Although some of the absorbed foreign words have retained the plural forms of their original languages, the tendency increasingly is to anglicize them.

Singular	Plural
	Anglicized Plurals:
appendix	appendixes
focus	focuses
memorandum	memorandums
stadium	stadiums
toyi-toyier	toyi-toyiers
	Foreign plurals:
alumna	alumnae
alumnus	alumni
beau	beaux
hypothesis	hypotheses

See: **Plural forms**

Four-letter words

1. These are, commonly, swear words. They are not acceptable in either informal or formal English, although they will be found inter alia in novels, short stories and plays when writers wish to create a particular atmosphere.

2. Modern dictionaries will include entries for many such words, usually indicating that they are slang as well as taboo (ie likely to cause shock or offence).

3. In some writing, such as newspaper reports, swear words will be quoted by inserting asterisks or dashes between the first and last letters of such words (eg f**k or s--t).

Fore-, for

1. **Fore-** is a suffix meaning 'in the front; before'.

> foreground
> foreleg

2. **For** is quite distinct from **fore-** and is used as a preposition.

> This money is for him.
> They left for Durban today.
> He paid for his course.
> He went to the farm for a holiday.
> Please do this for Charles.

Fragmentary sentence

1. A fragmentary sentence is a sentence which is grammatically incomplete. This is an error which should be avoided, especially in formal English where the writer is expected to display a command of grammar, style, and usage in every sentence The secret here is to write in complete sentences, expressing complete ideas.

2. A complete sentence can stand alone, whereas a fragmentary sentence cannot. However, some grammatically complete sentences do not make sense unless the reader knows what an earlier sentence states.

3. Pronouns may refer to a previous statement, but the sentence can still stand on its own.

> They showed it to us.

4. The auxiliary verbs, such as 'will' and 'can', may draw their meaning from verbs in preceding sentences.

> She can if you will.

5. Coordinating connectives and transitional phrases are frequently used to commence sentences, especially when the relationship with the preceding sentence is clear.

> For example, the price of petrol has gone up again.
> And they did exactly that.
> Thus, we see another example of gravy-train politics.

6. By contrast, a statement beginning with a subordinating connective (subordinating conjunctions, relative pronouns, and words such as 'that' and 'what') is not a sentence, even though the rest of the statement may be grammatically correct.

> X Although Jason invited me to his flat.
> X Because he wanted to show me his paintings.
> X What Shirley actually said after I got there.

7. Statements without a subject and a predicate are not sentences.

> X Demanding to be given an audience at once.
> X With congratulations to each and every one.

8. Fragmentary sentences are often those composed with non-finite verb forms.

> X I played the game and then going inside to shower.
>
> √ I played the game and then went inside to shower.

9. Fragmentary sentences often result from jumbled structures.

> X Most home-owners who sink a bore-hole to save on the costs of water, which is the main purposes of drilling.
>
> √ Most home-owners who sink a bore-hole to save on the costs of water, which is the main purpose for drilling, realize little financial gain.

10. Detached phrases or clauses are fragmentary sentences.

> X Bob bought a new lawn-mower. An electric model.

11. A detached dependent clause is a fragmentary sentence.

> X I didn't read the book. Because I didn't have time.
> √ I didn't read the book because I didn't have time.

See: **Sentences**

Fulfil

Confusion over the spelling arises because of the American practice of ending the word with a double -l. Other forms of this verb, which means 'to perform a duty or obligation', are spelt as follows: **fulfilment, fulfilling** and **fulfilled**.

See: **Spelling**

Full-stop (.)

A full-stop indicates the longest pause in reading and is used at the end of a sentence unless a question mark or exclamation mark is required.

See: **Abbreviations**

136

Fused sentences

1. Also known as 'run-on sentences' or 'run-together sentences', fused sentences occur when two independent clauses are joined together without any punctuation.

> X He is a good tutor the director is always singing his praises.

2. The remedy is to indicate the main break in the sentence by using the proper punctuation:

• With 'but', 'and', 'or', 'for', 'nor' —
Independent clause (comma + conjunction) independent clause

• Without 'but', 'and', 'or', 'for', 'nor' —
Independent clause (semi-colon) independent clause

> √ He is a good tutor, and the director is always singing his praises.
> √ He is a good tutor; the director is always singing his praises.

See: **Comma splice**

137

Gender

1. **Gender** is the term used to classify words as masculine, feminine or neuter.

2. In English there is no gender except for the third person singular pronoun – which has masculine (he), feminine (she), and neuter (it) – and the relative pronoun, which has who (masculine and feminine) and which (neuter).

3. There are some words which are altered or entirely replaced by other words according to the sex of the creature named.

See: **Sexist language**

4. The following list contains those words most frequently used.

Male	Female	Male	Female
bachelor	spinster	husband	wife
baron	baroness	lad	lass
boar	sow	landlord	landlady
bridegroom	bride	lord	lady
colt	filly	mayor	mayoress
dog	bitch	monk	nun
drake	duck	nephew	niece
duke	duchess	ram	ewe
earl	countess	sir	madam
emperor	empress	sire	dame
executor	executrix	stallion	mare
gander	goose	steer	heifer
god	goddess	testator	testatrix
heir	heiress	waiter	waitress
hero	heroine	widower	widow
host	hostess	wizard	witch

Generalizations

1. A generalization occurs when one jumps to a conclusion from insufficient evidence. One needs a large number of examples, or a representative sample, before one can make a generalization.

2. A particular kind of generalization depends on the use of stereotypes. A stereotype is a description or a standardized mental image which pays too much attention to characteristics supposedly common to a group, and not enough attention to individual differences. Statements which claim to be true about all members of a particular group are generally stereotypes, and therefore not objectively accurate or true.

> All white South Africans are conservative.
>
> Women are less intelligent than men.
>
> Black men are better lovers.
>
> Men are lazy slobs who would rather watch soccer than spend time with their families.
>
> Unisa students are dropouts who couldn't make the entrance requirements at other universities.

3. Generalizations should be avoided, especially when they are based on too few examples or on too little information.

> All generalizations are dangerous – including this one!

Genitive

The genitive is the possessive case. It is usually formed by adding 's to a singular noun, and an apostrophe ' to a plural noun.

139

> my sister's house
> my parents' house

See: **Apostrophe; Case; Possessive case**

Gerund

1. A gerund has the form of a participle but it acts as a noun.

> **Writing** at my desk is a pleasurable experience.
> As a boy he enjoyed **scuffing** the toes of his shoes.
> The tramp's only concern in life is **drinking**.
> He concentrates on **throwing** the ball.
> I like her **singing** very much indeed.

2. A gerund may also form a compound noun by combining with another noun.

> **running**-shoes *(shoes for running in)*
> **sleeping**-bag *(bag for sleeping in)*
> **swimming**-costume *(costume to wear when swimming)*

Got

1. When used to excess, this useful utility word can detract from written English. Got is the past tense form of get and means 'to acquire or obtain'. It is quite often incorrectly used in the sense of 'possession'.

> X My house has got a red roof
> √ My house has a red roof.
>
> *(The house has not obtained a red roof;*
> *the fact is that the roof of the house is red.)*

2. Such expressions are often used in spoken English, but **got** should be used sparingly in written English.

3. Begot, meaning 'to give existence to' and encountered in the older versions of the Bible, is no longer commonly used.

See: **Gotten**

Gotten

Although gotten is the older form, South African usage follows the British preference for **got**. Gotten will be found in some American speech and writing.

> He has gotten rid of the dog that bit the postman.

Grammar

Derived from the Greek word meaning 'the science of letters', grammar has come to mean the study or science of, or rules for the combination of words into sentences (syntax) and the forms of words (morphology).

For years the term meant a set of rules drawn up by English usage specialists: it was the aim of the scholarly and the educated to observe these rules. During this century developments in the field of linguistics have stressed that languages are dynamic and change despite laid-down rules. Nevertheless, if people are to understand each other they need to observe certain common rules of speaking and writing. Knowledge of the rules alone will not enhance communication; nor will reading significantly develop one's language skills. English must be used if it is to be learned properly.

This book deals with points of English grammar, style, and usage. However, under certain headings, specific points of grammar are explored: refer to the Index for a list of the headings which are of direct relevance to this topic.

H

Hang, hanged, hung

1. The past tense or past participle of the verb **hang** is **hung**.

> He hung his coat on the hook.
> She hung the curtains on the rail.

2. When the word is used to describe the result of implementing capital punishment or a death sentence, the past participle or past tense form that is used is **hanged**.

> She was hanged for murder.

Have

See: **Anomalous finite verbs**

Help

1. The verb help can be followed by an object and an infinitive verb, with or without 'to'.

> Can somebody help me to complete my tax form?
> I helped him compile the report.

2. **Help** can also be used without an object.

> Would you please help wash the dishes?

Homely, homily

1. **Homely**, in the sense of 'that which is simple but pleasant' (The house has a lovely homely atmosphere), should not be confused with **homily**, which is either a sermon, or a long and boring talk – usually concerning matters of behaviour.

2. **Homely** can also mean 'somewhat plain in appearance', and is often used as a euphemism for ugly.

Homonyms

These are words which sound similar (and are sometimes spelt similarly), but which have different meanings.

accept / except	compliment / complement
affect / effect	there / their
already / all ready	past / passed
altogether / all together	its / it's

See: Individual entries for each pair

However

1. This word has the same meaning as 'but'.

2. It should be used as near as possible to the beginning of a sentence because it serves as a transitional expression.

3. The word **however** signals the introduction of a contrasting conclusion or idea. It is therefore always marked off with a comma.

4. It aids understanding and adds to the continuity of your writing or speaking.

> I have been invited to the party. It is, however, not possible for me to be there.

> I am a chocolate addict. However, I need to limit my intake if I want to fit into my jeans.

See: **Transitions**

Hyperbole

A hyperbole is a figure of speech which employs dramatic overstatement or exaggeration for effect.

See: **Exaggeration; Understatement**

Hyphen (-)

1. A hyphen is used to join compound words.

> ex-policeman
> post-apartheid South Africa
> ice-cold drink

2. Hyphens are useful in clarifying the meanings of words.

> reform vs re-form
> recover vs re-cover
> forty-five two-rand coins

3. Hyphens also help to avoid awkward juxtaposition of letters.

> co-operate
> re-educate

4. **Hyphenation** refers to the breaking of words at the end of a line. The following rules apply to hyphenation:

   • Words should be broken between syllables.

> em-ploy-ment
> re-edu-ca-tion

See: **Syllables**

• A helpful hint to remember is that the portion of the word at the end of the line should give the reader a clue as to what is to follow. Avoid giving misleading or confusing pieces of the word.

> X reed-ucation

• When a word is made up of separate morphemes (units of meaning), the break should come between morphemes.

> to-morrow
> read-ing
> our-selves

• Do not ever break a word so that only one letter is left either at the beginning or the end of a line.

• Do not break words of one syllable, such as

burst   change   drink   through

See: **Syllables**

• Do not break a suffix of fewer than three letters from the rest of the word:

'-ing' may be separated
'-al', '-le', '-ly', and '-ed' endings may not be separated.

5. The hyphen should not be confused with the dash (—), which is longer, written with a space on either side, and indicates a pause.

See: **Dash**

I

ie

Meaning 'that is', **ie** is the short form of the Latin *id est*. This abbreviation is used in explanations. Sometimes it is confused with **eg** which is the abbreviation for *exempli gratia*, meaning 'for example', and which is used when quoting examples. Both of these abbreviations are usually preceded by a comma.

See: **viz**

Idioms

1. Idioms are like metaphors in that they are examples of the non-literal use of language. An idiom can be defined as a group of words whose meaning cannot be grasped from the normal meanings of the words that make up the idiom.

   For example, the literal meaning of the idiom 'to kick the bucket' gives no clue to the idiomatic meaning, namely 'to die'.

2. Idioms range from opaque to fairly transparent. Opaque idioms are less easy for non-native speakers to decipher. For example, an idiom such as 'a red herring' (meaning a false trail or misleading clue) is relatively opaque. The idiom actually derives from the custom of dragging a smoked herring across a trail to put hunting dogs off the scent of their quarry.

3. Any alteration in the form of the idiom tends to emphasize the idiom's literal meaning, and thus make it sound nonsensical. Therefore, idioms are fixed; that is, their form cannot be changed in the following respects:

- Number

Singular must be kept singular, plural must be kept plural.

> √ to burn one's boats
> X to burn one's boat
> *(destroy any means of escape or backing out of a situation)*
>
> √ a wild goose chase
> X a wild geese chase
> *(a fruitless errand or enterprise)*
>
> √ to sow one's wild oats
> X to sow one's wild oat
> *(to go through a young, reckless, and carefree period, probably characterized by sexual promiscuity)*

- Determiners

> √ kick the bucket *(to die)*
> X kick a bucket
>
> √ smell a rat *(notice something suspicious)*
> X smell the rat

- Word Order

> √ spick and span *(neat, tidy)*
> X span and spick
>
> √ thick and fast *(quickly)*
> X fast and thick

4. Idioms can usually not be translated from one language into another.

van die os op die jas gepraat ...
X speaking of the ox on the coat ...
(used when changing subjects abruptly)

moeng a dinaka di maripa
X a guest has short horns
(more or less equivalent to 'manners maketh the man')

imbuz' igudl' iguma
X the goat rubs itself on the door screen
(to describe circumlocution, or someone who does not get to the point)

izithupha ziy' emasini
X thumbs going for sour milk
(used to describe close friends)

5. Idioms are often clichéd in that they are tired and over-used. Because they lack precision and impact, they should be avoided in formal writing.

See: **Clichés**

If

See: **Whether**

If I were ...

We use special tenses with **if** in cases where we are talking about 'unreal' events that will probably not happen, or where we are making a tentative, speculative statement. This structure is called the 'conditional'.

If I were you, I would refuse to let him treat me that way.
If I were the manager, I would immediately crack down on long tea breaks.

> If I were a smoker, I would be very worried about my health.
> If you were to telephone at about six o'clock this evening,
>   you would probably find him at home.
> If I were to tell you the full story, you would never believe me.

See: **Auxiliary verbs**

Illusion

See: **Allusion**

Immigrate

See: **Emigrate**

Imperative

This is the name which is given to the form of the verb used for commands, prohibitions or requests.

> Shut the door. *(Command)*
> Don't talk inside. *(Prohibition)*
> Give me a pen, won't you? *(Request)*

See: **Mood**

Impersonal constructions

1. An impersonal construction is a subject-verb combination: the subject does not refer to anything named, specified or definite; little or no action is conveyed by the verb.

2. Impersonal constructions are useful when a writer wishes to eliminate personal opinions from a phrase or statement. Such phrases, however, lack force or conviction. When used too often the writing becomes weak, if not dull.

149

> It appears that he was delayed.
>
> It was said that many people were at the party.
>
> It looked as if his years of experience would prove useful in finding a solution.

3. Some impersonal constructions cannot be avoided.

> It is raining
>
> It is worthy of note.

4. Try when writing, to use more direct and forceful constructions.

> X It seems that she was late.
>
> √ She was late.

See: **Active, passive; One**

Implicit

This adjective means 'suggested' or 'unquestioning'.

See: **Explicit**

Imply, infer

Imply and infer are commonly confused.

1. **Imply** means to hint or suggest, while **infer** means to draw conclusions or make deductions from what is suggested.

2. **Implying** is thus something that a speaker or writer does, while **inferring** is something that the reader or listener does.

> The secretary implied by her tone of voice that she was irritated and overworked.

> The child inferred from his mother's expression that she was
> exasperated with him.

In-, un-

1. **In-** and **un-** are prefixes used to negate a word.

2. Usually words of Latin or French origin have **in-** ('indirect' or'
   invalid').

3. Words of Old English origin usually have **un-** ('untruth' or
   'unhurt').

There are many exceptions to these guidelines.

See: **Un-, in-**

Indefinite article

A or **an** are the indefinite articles.

See: **A; An; Articles**

Indirect speech

1. Indirect speech, also called reported speech, is used when we
   talk about what someone said – without using the exact words.
   We thus report something in our own words to give the
   substance of what was said.

> The receptionist asked the student whom he wanted to see.
> The student replied that he was waiting to see his personal tutor.

2. The tenses, word order, and pronouns may be different in
   reported speech from those used in direct speech.

> Direct: She said, 'I can't stand it any more.'
> Indirect: She said that she couldn't stand it any more.

> Direct: The doctor asked, 'How are you feeling?'
> Indirect: The doctor asked how I was feeling.

3. When the 'reporting' verb is in the past tense ('she said', 'he asked', 'we wondered') the verbs in the reported speech are also past.

> Direct: 'It may rain.'
> Indirect: She said that it might rain.

4. After a reporting verb in the past tense, the verbs in the reported speech may retain the original speaker's tense in cases when we are reporting things that are still true.

> She told me the other day that she is pregnant.

5. When the reporting verb is in the present tense, the verbs in the reported speech are usually the same tense as that used by the original speaker.

> Direct: 'What time is the meeting?'
> Indirect: He wants to know what time the meeting is.

See: **Direct speech**

Infinitive

1. An infinitive is a non-finite part of the verb and does not assert (or predicate) anything about the subject of a sentence. The simplest form of the verb is usually preceded by **to**.

> Doctor Khumalo tried **to catch** the ball.

2. The infinitive may function as a noun, adjective or adverb.

> **To run** is **to exercise** *(Subject and complement)*
> Use this wood **to burn**. *(Adjective)*
> We stopped **to rest** the horses. *(Adverb)*

3. The infinitive form of the verb (without **to**) is used with the auxiliary verbs – 'shall', 'will', 'should', 'would', 'do', 'may', 'might', 'can' and 'could' – to form the compound tenses.

> I shall travel by car.
> Both of us can play the game.

4. In addition to the anomalous finite verbs, there are a number of verbs which are usually followed by the infinitive. They include:

afford hope wish agree learn arrange manage begin mean care need dare offer decide plan do pretend endeavour promise expect refuse fear seem guarantee swear have want hesitate

5. A number of verbs can be followed by either the gerund or the infinitive:

bear love begin omit cease prefer continue regret forget remember hate need intend neglect learn start like try

6. A verb, such as 'expect', 'fear', 'hope', 'intend', 'like' or 'want', is followed by the infinitive as an object, and always expresses a time of action which occurs before the action conveyed by the infinitive.

> I plan **to run** in the Comrades Marathon.*(The plan exists before the actual date of the Comrades Marathon.)*
> I expect **to be finished** with this project by the end of the month. *(The expectation is in the present time; the project will be finished in the future.)*

7. Some verbs are not followed by the infinitive but by a gerund. Included in this group of verbs are the following:

admit	go on	advise	cannot help
avoid	imagine	consider	understand
include	contemplate	involve	continue
delay	mind	deny	keep
miss	detest	necessitate	dislike
postpone	endure	practise	enjoy
put off	escape	risk	excuse
report	face	set about	fancy
stop	finish	suggest	give up

See: **Anomalous finite verbs; Finite and non-finite verbs; Split infinitive**

In my opinion

This expression should be used when translating the Afrikaans expression 'na my mening' or 'volgens my'. 'According to me' or 'after my meaning' are direct translations, and meaningless in English.

Innuendo

An innuendo is a remark which contains a hidden insult or unacceptable suggestion; in other words, the speaker or writer wishes to suggest something without being open about the matter.

> You scored very highly in this test, as did Mary. You sit next to her, don't you?
> *(The innuendo, or implication, is that you cheated by copying her work.)*

Inside

A common mistake is to use the phrase **inside of** rather than **inside**.

> There are three bedrooms inside the house.

Instruction words

Essay topics are characterized by the use of 'instruction words' – verbs which tell you what you are expected to do with the topic, and how you should approach your task. Each subject has its particular favourites, and instruction words may mean slightly different things for different disciplines. Your lecturers in each subject field should be able to explain to you precisely what they mean when they say 'Describe ...' or 'Analyze ...'. Always approach your lecturer if you are unsure about what an assignment requires. The most commonly used instruction words are explained below:

Account for See Explain

Analyze
This word means that you should divide the topic into parts; define or label each part; show how the parts are related to each other; and examine each part carefully, systematically, and critically.

Assess See Evaluate

Compare
To examine the similarities and differences between two things, sometimes in terms of particular specified characteristics. The words 'relate', 'relative', or 'relationship' in an instruction also imply that a comparison is required. (As in: 'Discuss the relative importance of ...'.)

See: **Contrast**

Consider

To consider means to pay attention to the pros and cons of an argument.

Contrast

To look at the differences between two things. See Compare.

Criticize / Critical

To make a considered evaluation of a topic or phenomenon. Any judgements should be objectively substantiated and backed up with sound argument or evidence.

Describe

To describe something means to give a detailed account of its features and characteristics. Often, a listing of visible features with the purpose of supporting an argument, or proving some point.

Discuss

This is probably the most common instruction word used by lecturers. To 'discuss' does NOT imply a general chat about a topic. In academic terms, to discuss a topic means to investigate it thoroughly, using argument and reasoning. You are required to take a critical approach (that is, to look at all aspects of the issue, and to justify any statements you make).

Evaluate

To evaluate (or assess) something means that you have to present an opinion as to the value or usefulness usually of some theory or system. Any judgements or opinions must be backed up with sound supporting argument.

Explain

To explain (or account for) something, one needs to concentrate on causes or reasons for a particular event or phenomenon - to show why and how certain things are as they are.

Relate See Compare.

See: **Organization**

156

Intensifiers

1. Intensifiers are words that are used to strengthen adjectives, nouns, verbs, or adverbs.

> I am **very** happy.
> They are **extremely** dissatisfied.
> She is **really disgustingly** overweight.
> He is **most** unhappy.
> He is a **mere** child.

2. Overuse of intensifiers leads to wordiness rather than emphasis, and two intensifiers cannot usually be used together.

> X I am very much unhappy.

Interjections

These are words used to express emotions or feelings, such as surprise, anger, dismay. Their use is accompanied by an exclamation mark.

> **Ouch!** That hurt.
> **Oh no!** I've forgotten my code number.

Intransitive

See: **Transitive**

Introduction

The **introduction** to an essay is placed in the beginning paragraph, which introduces the reader to the subject of the

157

essay. It should contain a thesis statement which, in a single sentence, sets out the subject. The thesis statement is more inclusive than the topic sentences in each of the middle paragraphs.

> *Here is an example of a thesis statement from the introduction to P Roberts' Understanding English:*
>
> The history of English since 1700 is filled with many movements and counter-movements, of which we can notice only a couple. One of these is ...

See: **Essay, writing; Organization**

Inverted commas

See: **Quotation marks**

Irony

1. Irony is a rhetorical strategy, where the actual meaning is other than that which is stated. The simplest form of irony is sarcasm.

> Your 4-year old child knocks over a jug of milk so that it pours all over the kitchen floor. You exclaim 'What a clever thing to do!'
>
> *(Although the words sound like praise, they are actually critical. This contrast between what is said, and what is meant is what constitutes **irony**.)*

2. Situational irony arises from a contrast or difference between what we expect, and what happens. An event or situation turns out to be the reverse of what we expect.

-ise, -ize

1. A number of words derived from Latin have the **-ise** suffix. They include:

advertise	exercise	advise	revise
compromise	supervise	despise	surprise
devise			

2. There is a growing tendency to use the -ise ending, although there are a number of words ending in **-ize**, and the Americans opt for this ending.

See: **-ize, -ise**

Italics

Italics refers to a special kind of slanting type used to make words stand out in a text. (Underlining can be used instead if *italic* type is not available.) *Italics* (or underlining) can be used in the following cases:

1. To indicate use of a word considered foreign.

> *tête-a-tête*   *glasnost*

2. For titles of books, films, and theatre productions.

> *Lord of the Flies*   *Rambo IV*   *Boesman and Lena*

3. To focus attention on a word being discussed.

> *Misogamy* comes from two Greek roots; *misos* meaning hatred, and *gamos* meaning marriage.

4. For emphasis. (As with all emphatic devises, underlining or *italics* for emphasis should not be overused.)

159

> That is *exactly* the problem that we are trying to avoid.

Its, it's

1. **Its** is a possessive pronoun (as are 'his', 'hers', 'yours', 'ours', 'theirs', and 'my'/'mine').

> My telephone directory has lost half its pages
> Despite its disadvantages, this scheme is the best we've come up with so far.

2. **It's** is the contracted form of 'it is' and of 'it has'.

> It's hot today, isn't it?
> Although it's been a good year for the company, there is still room for improvement.

See: **Apostrophe; Homonyms**

-ize, -ise

1. The **-ize** ending is sometimes used for verbs derived from the Greek suffix *-zo*, which means 'to make, become, use or act like'.

> anaesthetize *(to make insensitive to pain)*
> italicize *(to use italics)*

2. The Americans tend to use -ize regardless of a word's origin. The Oxford English Dictionary is faithful to etymology and uses -ize on the basis of a word's origin.

3. As most -ize words can be spelled **-ise**, the use of the suffix -ise is possibly the safest option.

See: **-ise, -ize.**

160

J

Jargon

Jargon is language containing technical words or expressions that pertain to a particular trade or discipline. Jargon may be used, and understood, in communications between specialists sharing a common interest in or knowledge of a discipline. However, when the communication is between specialist and non-specialist, understanding and comprehension are likely to be hindered by the use of jargon.

Sport

Rugby:	prop forward, hooker, drop-kick, try.
Soccer:	goalie, right back, off-side, small box.
Tennis:	net, love, deuce, foot-fault, tram-lines.

Law

Affidavit, commissioner of oaths, swear, cross-examine, subpoena, identikit, jurisprudent, *de jure*, the Bar, delict.

Economics

Bull and bear markets, stock, shares, yield, heated, prime rate, supply-side, gearing, turn-over, shrinkage.

Medical

Cardiac arrest, mandible, X-ray, CAT scan, placebo, dispense, generic, aids, prognosis, fracture, myopic.

Travel

Side-slip, bucket seat, stabilizers, ETA, eco-tourism, B & B, safari, jet-lag, economy class, three-star accommodation.

Publishing

Galley proofs, blue pencil, remainder, font, stitch, plates, royalties, copyright, inspection copy, 8-point, spot-colour.

> **Education**
> Affective objectives, OHP, infant teacher, remediation, pedagogical, cybernetics, multidisciplinary, ergonomics, colloquium, university chair.

Justify

See: **Motivate**

Juxtapose

When two things are placed side by side, they are juxtaposed. It is a term used quite frequently in literary analysis especially when considering the effects of having two things, such as consecutive stanzas in a poem, in the state of being placed side by side or in juxtaposition to one another.

> When his works are considered in juxtaposition with those of Shakespeare's contemporary dramatists, his extraordinary contribution to literature becomes apparent.

K

Kind

1. **Kind** is singular, and if used as the subject of a verb, should take a singular verb. It also takes a singular pronoun.

> Kites of **this** kind are superbly balanced.
> This kind of kites **is** superbly balanced.
>
> BUT
>
> X These kind of kites are superbly balanced.

2. The reason for the error above is that we conceive of a number of examples of one type. Forgetting that **kind** is singular we use the plural 'these'. In written English we have enough time to avoid the error.

See: **Agreement**

Kind of

See: **Sort of**

Kwazulu-Natal

This name refers to one of the regions demarcated in terms of the 1994 interim constitution in South Africa. There is often doubt as to whether a capital Z should be used. This problem is a consequence of using the prefix **kwa** from the source language. In Zulu, the practice is to retain the capital for the root-form of the word when it is preceded by a prefix and to use the lower case to start the word: *amaZulu*. When writing the name in English, the practice is to anglicize the prefix by starting it with an upper case **K** and also using the lower case **z** for the root-form. As is the norm with double-barrelled names, the second name retains the upper case **N** after the hyphen.

See: **Capital letters; Foreign words**

L

Language, changes in

Spoken languages are repeatedly experimenting with new words, and expressions are often borrowed from other languages. Changes in technology, modes of living and new interests all introduce items of vocabulary and expressions into speech. Examples in South Africa are words such as 'hassle' and 'necklace', both of which have acquired new meanings and even acceptance in written English.

> The management faced a number of hassles on the shopfloor.
> 'I felt hassled,' the student said.
> The horrific incident resulted in the death by necklacing of three women.
> He was necklaced despite his protestations.

Borrowing is particularly prevalent in South Africa where numerous languages are spoken. Words such as 'trek' have long been accepted in English; a more recent addition is 'apartheid'. In colloquial English, words that are often used include 'lekker', 'indaba', 'donga', 'dop', 'zol', 'toyi-toyi', 'induna', 'krans', 'ubuntu' and many more. Some words enjoy wider acceptance than others.

Latter, the

The latter refers to the second of two things mentioned.

> Console and Themba soon arrived, the latter wearing his
> university tie.

Lay, lie

Lay and lie are often confused.

1. **Lay** means to put down carefully or to put down flat. It is declined as follows: 'to lay', 'laying', and 'laid'.

> 'Please start laying the table.'
> 'But it's not my turn to lay the table, I laid it yesterday.'

2. **Lay** always has an object.

> to lay the table
> to lay an egg
> to lay the papers out

3. **Lie** means to be horizontal, to be down flat. It is declined as follows: 'to lie', 'laying', 'lay' and 'lain'.

> 'Why do you need to go and lie down again? You are always just lying around!'
> 'I only lay down for half an hour this morning. Don't exaggerate!'
> 'Well your bed looks as if it has been lain on for days.'

4. **Lie** does not have a direct object.

5. **A lie** (noun) is a falsehood or an untruth.

Learn, learned, learnt

1. The past tense and past participle forms are learned or learnt.

Fewer people now use **learnt** but it is still encountered as a past participle. **Learned** as a single-syllable word predominates for the past tense and increasingly in the past participial forms.

> I have not yet learned whether she arrived safely.
> When learnt/learned by heart a speech often strikes the listener as dull and uninspired.

2. The two-syllabled participial adjective 'learned' is used to describe someone who is widely read and erudite.

> My learned friend is a fine lawyer.

Learn, teach

1. Unlike the Afrikaans 'leer', learn and teach have different meanings. To **learn** means to study or to receive knowledge. To **teach** means to impart knowledge to someone else.

2. The Afrikaans influence means that learn, which sounds closer to the Afrikaans 'leer', is often misused. 'To learn a person something' has come to be regarded as illiterate speech. It was once viewed as good English and is, for example, encountered in early English versions of the Bible.

> X She learnt me a lesson I shall never forget.
> √ She taught me a lesson I shall never forget.

3. **Learning** is something that the learner (a student or pupil, for example) does, while **teaching** is something that the teacher or instructor does.

> I am going to learn how to drive a car.
> I shall be quite happy to teach you how to drive.

167

Lend, borrow

1. The influence of Afrikaans often causes confusion between these two words. In Afrikaans there is only one word 'leen' which means both **lend** and **borrow**. In English the differences are distinct. The person who owns the item **lends** it. The person who does not own the item, but who wants to use it, **borrows** it.

> Dad, may I borrow your car?
> Yes, but I can lend it to you only until this evening. I need it to go a meeting tonight.
>
> A toy library lends toys. Mothers may borrow them for periods of two weeks, and then have to return them.

2. To confuse matters still further the Afrikaans word 'leen' also means 'loan', which in English is used in a different context.

> That book is on loan from the library.

Less, fewer

See: **Fewer, less**

Letter writing

1. **Business letters** should be simple, clear and to the point. Write so that the person receiving the letter understands what you are saying. Therefore, avoid the clichés, elaboration and convoluted expressions so often associated with business letters. Use direct, uncluttered English.

2. Think before you write. Make notes and be certain that you know what you wish to say before drafting your letter. A useful plan to follow includes these points:

- State the fact/s with which the letter is concerned.
- Develop the fact/s so as to outline the problem, or to pose a question.
- Suggest a solution to the problem or question.
- Offer a solution by stating what you intend doing or suggesting what the receiver ought to do.
- Conclude your letter politely.

3. Try to write logically, honestly, helpfully and succinctly.

4. Follow your business's house rules for layout, referencing, spelling, abbreviations, hyphenation, use of job titles and letter endings. Should there be no house rules some useful guidelines are as follows:

- Block addresses and paragraphs, salutations, subject lines, and endings.
- Hyphenate where natural breaks occur or where the break makes sense as two separate words or syllables, and where pronunciation is aided.

See: **Hyphenation**

- Letters should be signed by the individual whose name and job title are clearly typed beneath the signature.

See: **Business writing**

5. **Personal letters** are so varied in content, style and tone, as well as so flexible in format, that no complete description of every type of personal letter is possible here. In short, depending upon the familiarity which exists between you and the receiver, almost anything is acceptable. Like the business letter, a personal letter should be simple, clear, courteous and to the point.

The following guidelines may be useful:

- The return address and date are positioned to the right at the top of the page.
- Begin the salutation on the left, a line or two below the date.

169

- The body of the letter comprises at least one paragraph.
- A polite, complimentary close occurs two or more lines below the rest of the letter.
- The writer's signature, name or nickname is placed below the closing.

Licence, license

1. **Licence** is a noun meaning 'leave or permission', or 'a permit of some kind'.

2. **License** is a verb meaning 'to allow, to grant permission'.

3. As with the advice / advise and practice / practise distinction, a very simple memory aid will help ensure that you never use the incorrect spelling.

> Just as **n** (for noun) comes before **v** (for verb) in the alphabet, so **c** comes before **s**.
> Therefore the noun is spelt with a **c**, and the verb with an **s**.

Lie, lay

Be careful not to confuse these two words. **Lay** always needs an object.

> We lie down to sleep.
> We lay down the books we are carrying.

See: **Lay, lie**

Like, as

1. **Like** is a preposition. It is used to say that certain things are similar.
   Like is always used before a noun or pronoun.

> You look like your sister.
> He ran like the wind.

2. **Like** is very often incorrectly used as a conjunction in conversational English. It is best to use **as** or **as if** in such sentences.

> X If you smoke like I do, you'll die young.
> √ If you smoke, as I do, you'll die young
>
> X I felt like I was being fooled.
> √ I felt as if I was being fooled..

3. **As** is a conjunction, and is used before clauses, and phrases beginning with a preposition. (See the above examples.)

Loan

The Afrikaans word 'leen' has several meanings, one of which is **loan**. The word means one has the use of something as the borrower.

> I have the loan of his car.

See: **Lend, borrow**

Logic

1. Logic demands that similar constructions be used to express similar ideas.

> X This is an important essay and which must be based on careful research.
>
> √ This is an important essay, and one which must be based on careful research.

It is important to bear in mind that, although you know what you mean, the reader has to depend on what has actually been said.

2. Logic may also be absent from writing when it contains too many abstract words; an over-abundance of generalizations; a *non sequitur*; and terms that are not properly defined:

• **Abstract words** such as 'truth' or 'fear' need to relate directly to the subject.

• **Generalizations** are broad statements covering a number of incidences and as such can land one in the 'logic trap' (for example, the statement that 'women have no mathematical ability' is clearly illogical; 'some women have no mathematical ability' is obviously not).

See: Generalizations

• A **non sequitur** (from the Latin, meaning 'it does not follow') occurs when a conclusion does not follow the argument on which it is based.

> We bought the rare kist for her dowry long ago, since it was made of stinkwood.
>
> *This is a non sequitur because the fact that the kist is made of stinkwood does not provide a logical reason (1) for buying the kist in the first place, or (2) for buying it long ago.*

• An undefined term, such as 'nationalism', will contribute to an absence of logic if the writer fails to explain exactly what he or she means by it – the reader might have a different understanding of what the word means.

Loose, lose

1. **Loose** (pronounced with an 's' sound as in 'goose') is an adjective meaning 'slack or relaxed'. 'To loosen' is a verb

which means 'to untie or to make less tight'.

2. **Lose** (pronounced with a 'z' sound as in 'booze') is a verb meaning 'to suffer loss', or 'to be deprived of something'.

> I always lose my keys. I have lost them twice this week.
> Please loosen the rope.
> This belt is too loose.

Lot of, many

1. **Many** is an adjective signifying 'a great number of' and should be used in preference to **lot of** in formal writing.

> Many languages are spoken in South Africa.

2. **A lot of**, meaning 'a large quantity of' or 'great number of', is used in informal contexts.

> He has a lot of work to catch up.

M

Main verbs

See: **Sentences**

Mainly

This is used today to mean 'in the main', 'for the most part'.

> He was mainly responsible for our raise in salary.

Malapropism

Malapropism is used to describe a ridiculous error made by someone who tries to use long, impressive words, but gets them laughably wrong.

> 'Please hurry, I extort you.' *(exhort)*
> Comparisons are odorous. *(odious)*

The word is derived from the French *mal à propos* meaning 'ill-suited to the purpose'.

Many, much

1. **Many** is used before countable nouns. It is the more acceptable form alternative to 'a lot of'.

> You made many mistakes in your essay.
> Many people are dissatisfied with their monthly pay cheque.
> How many circulars should I print?

2. **Much** is used before uncountable nouns.

> I haven't got much time.
> There has been much research into the problem of hyperactivity.

See: **Lot of, many; Nouns**

Margin

The space to the left of a sheet of paper is known as the **margin**, and should be left blank.

Mathematics

The abbreviation follows British usage (**maths**), rather than the American (math).

May, might

May and **might** are auxiliary verbs.

1. They are both used to ask for permission, although **might** is more tentative and hesitant.

> 'May I use the car tonight?'
> 'No, you may not.'
>
> 'I wonder if I might use your telephone?'

2. **May** is used to give or refuse permission.

Passengers may not smoke on domestic flights.
You may submit more than one competition entry.

3. **Might** can be used as the past tense of **may** in reported speech.

The secretary said that I might wait in her office.

4. **May** and **might** are used to talk about a possibility. **Might** is more tentative, and not quite as strong a possibility as **may**.

I may be able to help you.
It may be warm enough to swim by midday.
I might be home early, but don't bank on it.

5. **May** and **might** can be used with perfect tenses to indicate a possibility that past events happened.

'Why was Winnie not at the meeting?'
'She may have forgotten to come.'

Driving at 180 km an hour was a really dangerous thing to do –
you might have caused an accident!

6. 'Might of' written instead of 'might have' is an error caused by careless pronunciation.

See: **Can, may; Contractions**

Memorandum (Memo)

See: **Business writing**

Memoirs

See: **Autobiography**

Metaphor

A **metaphor** is a figure of speech in which one phenomenon is identified with another because of some point of similarity. The chief use of a metaphor, as with most figures of speech, is to make the abstract concrete and vivid by helping the reader to visualize it. A metaphor also helps to highlight, focus, and intensify certain aspects of an idea, concept, or object that the writer wants to emphasize in order to make communication with readers more effective.

Metaphors are most obvious in poetry and literature, but are also used in non-fictional writing.

> Idealism is the noble toga that political gentlemen drape over their will to power.
>
> (Aldous Huxley)
>
> Hiroshima was no longer a city but a burnt out prairie.
>
> (Michihiko Hachiya)
>
> Communism is not love. Communism is a hammer which we use to crush the enemy.
>
> (Mao Tse-Tung)

In constructing metaphors, one must make sure that the word picture one makes is clear. **Mixed metaphors** are word pictures that combine too many elements, thus creating inconsistent and conflicting messages which only confuse your reader.

> 'A diamond is withering away'
>
> Gauteng premier Tokyo Sexwale, on singer Brenda Fassie's admission that she had a cocaine addiction.
>
> *(Can a diamond 'wither away'?)*

Dead metaphors are word pictures that have lost their appeal and impact through overuse. They have become such common expressions that they no longer call up any images. Many clichés are dead metaphors.

> Raining cats and dogs
> Kill two birds with one stone
> Opening up a can of worms

See: **Analogy; Clichés; Simile**

Metre

1. Metre is the recognisably regular rhythm of a line of verse. It is evident in the basic pattern formed by the use of stressed and unstressed syllables. Many of the terms mentioned below are not vital in the accurate analysis or description of poetry. However, the recognition of these components and their effects is important.

2. The basic unit of metre is a **foot** and comprises two or three syllables; the patterns formed by the syllables each have technical names.

• Amphibrach
Two unstressed syllables interspersed by a stressed syllable

> Oŭr búglĕs

• Anapaest
Two unstressed syllables followed by a stressed syllable

> ĭntĕrvéne

• Dactyl
A stressed syllable followed by two unstressed syllables

> táke hĕr ŭp/téndĕrlў

• Iamb
An unstressed syllable followed by a stressed syllable

> ălóng

• Spondee
Two accented syllables mostly used as a variation in a single line.

> Rócks, Cáves,/Lákes, Féns,/Bógs, Déns,/ ănd shádes/ŏf Déath

• Trochee
A stressed syllable precedes an unstressed syllable.

> súnsĕt

The adjectives for the various feet listed above are spelled as follows:
amphibrachic, anapeastic, dactylic, iambic, spondaic and trochaic.

3. When a line of verse is marked off into feet, the line has been scanned. **Scanning** requires the identification of the kind of feet used in the line as well as the number of feet. There are technical terms for identifying the metrical length of lines.

   • Monometer – one foot
   • Dimeter – two feet
   • Trimeter – three feet
   • Pentameter – five feet
   • Hexameter – six feet (also called Alexandrine)
   • Heptameter – seven feet
   • Octameter – eight feet

A line of verse can thus be given a technical description once it has been scanned. Scansion depends on the development of a feeling for the rhythm as a basic pattern, which is seldom evident for long without a variation. Probably the most often encountered metre is **iambic verse**.

4. Not all lines of verse end with a complete foot: some lines end with a monosyllabic foot termed a **catalectic line**. Some lines contain an extra syllable or foot and are called **hypermetric**.

5. A last point of note is spelling: **metre** is a unit of length, while **meter** is a measuring device.

See: **Rhyme; Rhythm**

Millennium

1. The word **millennium** means a period of one thousand years. As the end of the second of the two millenniums, since the start of the Christian era, approaches and as the third millennium commences on 1 January 2001, the word will inevitably be used more frequently.

2. Write **second millennium** and **third millennium**, not Second Millennium nor 3rd Millennium.

3. The word is also used figuratively to mean a future time of prosperity and happiness for all people. People who believe that such a period will dawn are called **millenarians**. This figurative use of the word millennium is unrelated to the lapse of a period of one thousand years.

See: **Dates; Abbreviations; Numbers**

Misplaced modifier

This is a modifier which is acceptable and has something to modify; it is merely in the wrong place. (A dangling modifier, on the other hand, sometimes does not logically fit anywhere.)

A good hint is that a modifier should be placed as near as possible to that which it modifies.

> X I have been looking forward to studying this handbook for a long time.
>
> √ I have [for a] long [time] been looking forward to studying this Handbook.

See: **Dangling modifier; Modifier**

Misused words

Many words lose clarity of meaning through misuse.

1. **Alibi** means that one was in another place at the time of an alleged act. Colloquially it is used in the sense of an excuse.

See: **Alibi**

2. **Awful** means terrible or dreadful. Colloquially it has come to be used to mean very bad, very great or very much.

See: **Awful, awfully**

> I'm awfully sorry.
> I'm awfully glad.

3. **Fantastic** means wild, strange or grotesque. Through misuse it has a colloquial meaning of wonderful or marvellous.

See: **Fantastic**

> We had a fantastic holiday.

4. **Terrible** means something which causes great fear or horror. Misused, it sometimes means 'extremely'.

See: **Terrible**

> That's terribly kind of you.

Mixed metaphor

See: **Metaphor**

Modifier

1. A modifier is a word that affects the meaning of the verb or noun that it describes, limits or intensifies.

> The **green** jersey belongs to Susan.

2. A modifier can also be made up of a group of words.

> **Considering the circumstances**, he was lucky to pass.

See: **Dangling modifier; Misplaced modifier**

Moment in time

See: **Point in time**

Mood

Mood refers to the manner in which a verb is used.

1. **Indicative mood**
Here the verb is used to make a statement or ask a question.

> The meeting **will be held** on Monday.
> **Did** you **pass** the exam?

2. **Imperative mood**
Here the verb is used to make a request or give a command.

> **Bring** me the file, please
> **Stop** doing that!

3. Subjunctive mood

Here the verb is used to talk about possible events, to express a wish, condition, or hypothesis.

> If I **were** you, I **would refuse** to take responsibility for his mistakes.
> I **wish** it **were** Friday already.
> If smoking **were to be proved** harmless, more people **would smoke**.
> We **insist** that the culprit **be found** and punished.

More, most

1. **More**, the comparative form of 'many' and 'much', is used as an adjective.

> I have more work to do than he has.

2. It is also used as an adverb.

> He will be able to do his work more easily than Zinzi will.

3. **Most** is the superlative form of 'many' and 'much', and is often preceded by the article, 'the'.

> Who has done the most work?

4. The positive, comparative, and superlative forms are as follows:

many more most   much more most

Motivate

Motivate is often confused with the word 'justify'. Notice that the words have distinctly different meanings.

> He was motivated by the desire to succeed.
> You will find it hard to justify the fact that you did not do the work.

Mr, Mrs, Ms, Dr

1. The first letter of these titles always takes a capital and there is no full-stop after them.

2. **Mr** is the title prefixed to the surname (and first name) of a man, while **Mrs** is the title used for a married woman.

> Mr (George) Mgomezulu
> Mrs (Katrina) Oberholzer

3. **Ms** is the title prefixed to the surname (and first name) of a woman who is married or unmarried, and is pronounced [Miz] as in the first syllable of 'miserable'. **Miss** is the title often still used in South Africa for an unmarried woman.

> Ms Lephalala
> Miss Ngengebule

4. **Dr** is an abbreviation for debtor, doctor and drive (road). When **Dr** is used as the title for a married man, his wife does not in English acquire the right to the title.

See: **Salutation; Protocol**

Must

See: **Anomalous finite verbs**

My meaning

The correct expression is 'my opinion'.

See: **In my opinion**

185

N

Narrative

A narrative tells of events. The terms narrative poetry and narrative composition are used to describe writing which tells a story.

When writing a narrative, select the events you need to include, perhaps playing down less interesting points and expanding important episodes. Direct speech at dramatic moments enhances a story.

See: **Dialogue**

Need

See: **Anomalous finite verbs**

Negatives

Although the two most common negatives are 'no' and 'not', negation can also be indicated by adverbs such as 'never', 'nowhere', 'scarcely' and 'rarely', and by pronouns such as 'none', 'no-one', 'nobody' and 'nothing'.

The position of a negative in a sentence is important as everything after the negative words is generally negated.

> I still have not got the pen.
> *(I have never had the pen.)*
>
> I have not still got the dog.
> *(I do not have the dog now, although I had it once.)*

Note: Although it is used in Afrikaans, the double negative *(nobody knows nothing)* is unacceptable in English.

Neither ... nor

1. **Neither ... nor** are correlative conjunctions, used to balance two negative ideas. ('Both ... and' balance two positive ideas.)

> Neither the cleaner nor the security guard saw anyone in the building.
> I neither drink nor smoke.

2. Two singular subjects should be followed by a singular verb, although in informal writing, two singular subjects are sometimes followed by a plural verb.

> Neither my son nor my daughter likes going to the dentist.
> Informal:
> Neither the lecturer nor the student were happy with the finished assignment.

3. In formal writing, as with 'both ... and', and 'either ... or', and 'not only ... but also', structures using **neither ... nor** should be balanced – a noun with a noun, a verb with a verb, or an adjective with an adjective.

> X He is neither clever nor is he good looking.
>   (adj)   (clause)
> √ He is neither clever nor good-looking.
>   (adj)   (adj)

Neuter

The word neuter means neither masculine nor feminine.
Names in English have no gender even though there are some

words such as 'actress' or 'goddess' or 'squaw' or 'hind' which are used to denote the sex of the person or animal in question.

As English is an uninflected language, the neuter gender is irrelevant and survives only in the pronouns **it** and **which**.

See: **Gender; Sexist language**

Nobody, no-one

Nobody and **no-one** mean 'not a single person'.

Both these words are singular. In formal writing, they therefore take singular verbs, and pronouns referring to them must also be singular.

> Nobody likes his morals being questioned.
> No-one enjoys being criticized.

In informal writing or speech, the tendency is to treat the words as plurals and to use the pronoun 'they', rather than the masculine 'his'.

> No-one wears pantyhose in high summer unless they are forced to.
> Nobody likes to be caught with their hair in curlers.

See: **Anybody, anyone; Everybody, everyone, every; Sexist language**

None

1. **None** can mean 'not one'. In this case it takes a singular verb.

> Of the three applicants, none was really suitable.
> I submitted three proposals, but none was accepted.

2. **None** can also mean 'not any of'. In this case, with a plural noun, a plural verb is used.

> None of these pictures appeal to me.
> None of her friends support her crazy schemes.

3. **None** can also be used alone as a pronoun.

> 'How many of your exams did you pass?' – 'None!'
> Of the three meetings held last week I attended none.

4. Do not confuse **none** (not one) with 'no-one' (nobody).

Not only ... but also

1. **Not only ... but also** are correlative conjunctions which balance two equivalent positive statements.

> I not only arrived at work early, but also stayed late.

2. The structures should be balanced, in that two nouns, or two verbs, or two similar clauses, for example, are correlated.

> He writes not only novels, but also poetry.
>   (noun)   (noun)
>
> He not only disagreed with my ideas, but also attacked my character.
>   (clause)   (clause)

3. **Not only ... but also** is used for emphasis, and like all emphatic devices should not be overused. A simple 'and' is often adequate.

Nothing

1. **Nothing** (no + thing) is a singular noun and takes a singular verb.

189

> Nothing is as frustrating as having an automatic teller close down on you.

2. **Nothing** should not be used with another negative in the sentence.

> X I didn't do nothing. (Rather: I didn't do anything.)
> X I don't want nothing. (Rather: I don't want anything.)

See: **Negatives**

Nouns

Nouns are those words which are used to name people, things or qualities. Some nouns can be used in the plural form, most often formed by adding -s or -es, but others cannot. Many nouns have several meanings, only some of which may have plural forms.

• Countable nouns have both singular and plural forms.

> a cow, six cows
> a desk, many desks

• Uncountable nouns do not have plural forms and can be used in the singular form with words like 'enough', 'much', 'more' or 'some'. These nouns cannot be used with 'a', 'an', 'another', 'many', or with numbers.

> patriotism   deceit   hatred

• Some nouns can be used as countable or uncountable nouns.

> 'Three **teas** please.'   'Have some **tea**.'

Nouns are usually marked C (countable) or U (uncountable) in dictionaries.

See: **Number**

Novel

1. As a noun, **novel** means 'a longish work of prose telling a story' (eg *The Conservationist*).

2. As an adjective, **novel** means 'new'.

Number

Number refers to the difference between singular and plural.

1. Nouns have to agree with their pronouns in number.
   A singular noun takes a singular pronoun; a plural noun takes a plural pronoun.

> Singular:
> The boy ran down the street. **He** was late for **his** music lesson.
> The cat demanded attention from **its** owner.
>
> Plural:
> The boys taunted **their** classmate – **they** found his outfit ridiculous.

2. Subjects have to agree with their verbs in number.
   A singular subject takes a singular verb; a plural subject takes a plural verb.

> Singular:
> The boy, panting and out of breath, **runs** down the street.
>
> Plural:
> The boys, panting and out of breath, **run** down the street.
> The lecturer and the student **are** both responsible for successful education.

3. It is often not easy to decide whether a noun is 'one thing' (singular), or 'more than one thing' (plural). Nouns are usually marked C (countable) or U (uncountable) in dictionaries. Uncountable nouns have no plural and always take a singular verb.

> Their health is good.
> This advice is free.
> The information is useful.
> Travel broadens the mind.
>
> (Other uncountable nouns include 'progress', 'research', 'news', 'hair' and 'furniture'.)

4. Some nouns are always plural, and always take plural verbs and pronouns.

> 'Where are the scissors?' – 'They are in the kitchen.'
> 'Can't you mend these pants? They're full of holes.'

Numbers

In most instances Arabic numerals are used for numbers, although Roman numerals are still used in certain circumstances. Numbers are written in words in ordinary writing.

1. Addresses

> 123 Madiba Drive, Menlo Park, Mokonjane, 3007
>
> 35 Uhuru Apartments
> 123 Madiba Drive
> Menlo Park
> Mokonjane
> 3007

P O Box 432
Springs
1560

2. Dates

1 January 1999
the 1st of January 1999

October the thirteenth, 1873

3 000 BC BUT AD 35

1999 OR '99

3. Decimals

South African usage follows European usage: instead of the
decimal point, a comma is used. Large numbers are made
clearer by the use of spaces.

0,7
27,89
380,192

1 226 443,26
1 129,347

4. Money

In general avoid the use of the symbols 'R c' in prose text.
However, if they are used, figures should be used with them:
R27 not twenty-seven R. The decimal point is used in
monetary values – not the comma.

R27.35
R2 735.11

The anglicization of the word Rand has led to the correct usage in the plural form.

> The book costs eleven Rands.

5. Numbered paragraphs

Number paragraphs according to the following pattern.

> | 1. | Text of first paragraph commences. |
> |---|---|
> | 1.1 | First sub-point is discussed. |
> | | There is no full-stop after the last number for sub-paragraphs. |
> | 1.2 | Second sub-point commences. |
> | 1.2.1 | A further sub-division can occur. |
> | 1.2.2 | Sequential numbering continues ... |
> | 2. | The second paragraph or main point begins . |

The points can be blocked (as above) or indented:

> 1. Text of first paragraph commences.
>   1.1   First sub-point is discussed.
>   There is no full-stop after the last number for sub-paragraphs.
>   1.2   Second sub-point commences.
>   1.2.1   A further sub-division can occur.
>   1.2.2   Sequential numbering continues ...
> 2. The second paragraph or main point begins .

6. References

> II Henry IV: III (ii), 42
>
> *Were we to write out the above reference in full, we would state:*
>
> Henry IV, Part II, Act 3, Scene 2, Line 42.

- pp 6-7 refers to a continuous subject stretching over two pages, whereas pp 6, 7 indicates that the subject is mentioned disconnectedly on two successive pages.
- Figures are also used in statements identifying part of a book:

> 'The point is made tellingly in paragraph 4, lines 1-4, on p 119 of *The Sayings of Mao Tse-Tung*.'

8. Telephone numbers

> (012) 716-4218
> (03712) 28-3406

8. Time

Since metrication, the twenty-four hour clock notation has been the norm.

> 12:10 (ten minutes past midday.)
> 13:35 (twenty-five minutes to two o'clock.)

9. Travel details

> SAA flight SA 531 boards at gate 8.
> The N3 by-pass links with the R22 carriageway.

10. Words for numbers

Never begin sentences with numerals.

In descriptive matter, numbers up to and including one hundred are written in words.

In some specific instances it is also best to write out the numbers.

When writing out fractions, use a hyphen.

Four hundred people were present.

the seven dwarfs
she is nineteen years old
the twentieth century
his sister was ten times happier
a two-year-old

'I have said so a thousand times!'

With God a thousand years are but as one day.

two-thirds
one and three-quarters

the twentieth century
the twenty-first century

See: **Dates**

O

Object

1. An object is a noun or pronoun which completes the action of a transitive verb.

> We sold **the house**.
> We gave away **the kittens**.

2. The **direct object** answers the question 'who?' or 'what?' after the verb.

> The doorbell rang. Moolman opened **it**. A stranger greeted **him**. Moolman shuddered. He knew **that face**. The guest smiled. She entered **the hallway**. She shut **the door**. She pulled out **a knife**. Moolman froze. His guest laughed. Moolman grabbed **his kierie**. He attacked **his guest**. The knife went spinning. The woman grabbed **the doorknob**. She opened **the door**. She ran. Moolman slammed **the door** closed. He turned. He saw **his wife**. She had **a gun**. She fired.

3. The **indirect object** tells us to whom or for whom something was done. It may come between the verb and the direct object, or after the direct object.

> We sold the house **to a friend**.
> We gave away the kittens **to whomever wanted them**.
> The patient told **the psychologist** his dream.
> Eve gave **Adam** the apple.

> I taught **those children** a lesson they won't forget.
>
> I owe **Joseph** money.
>
> I bought the chocolates **for you**.

Occurred

The verb 'to occur' takes a double 'r' in the past tense and the present participle. (This avoids confusion with 'cured' and 'curing'.)

> The incident occurred on Tuesday.
>
> The occurrence was very distressing.

Of

1. **Of** has several meanings, including:

   - belonging to — This house is the property of Mr Moletsane.
   - away from — We are now within 5 km of Mamelodi.
   - after — Within a year of his mother's death his father died.
   - made by — The poems of Dylan Thomas are well known.

2. Use 'from' or 'off' rather than 'off of'.

> He jumped from the horse.
>
> He jumped off the train.

3. Where possible avoid the wordy phrase, 'on the part of'.

Older

Older is the comparative form of the word 'old'.

> My copy of the novel is an older edition than yours.

Older is not used when describing family relationships: the word **elder** is used.

See: **Elder**

On, onto

1. **On** is a preposition of place used for position on a line.

> His farm is on the way from Van Reenen's Pass to Ladysmith.
> Port Elizabeth is on the eastern coast of South Africa.

2. **On** is also used for position on a flat surface.

> Supper's on the table.
> The newspaper is on the bed.
> Pictures hang on a wall.

3. **On** is also a preposition of time used to indicate a particular day.

> Phone me on Saturday.
> My birthday's on June 23rd.
> We saw many old friends on our wedding day.

4. While 'on' refers to the position of something (with no movement), **onto** and **on to** are used when we describe movement towards a position.

Onto introduces a prepositional phrase, while **on to** introduces an adverbial phrase. **Onto** is more often used to describe an action completed in one short motion, while **on to** describes a longer, more progressive movement. When in doubt, rather use **on to.**

> The cat jumped onto the table.
> She threw her book onto the floor.
> Let us move on to our next topic.

One

One, as an impersonal pronoun, is used when the speaker wishes to be detached from what is being said or else wishes to make the statement less direct. If the statement is impersonally phrased, the result is less likely to be reactionary.

> One must consider the facts carefully before one decides on a course of action.

The possessive form is **one's**. (Note the apostrophe, unlike in the case of 'yours', 'hers', 'theirs', 'its' and 'ours'.)

See: **Impersonal constructions**

Only

Only should be used with care when it is to operate as an adverb.

> I saw only Mirriam at the station. *(The only person I saw there was Mirriam.)*
> I only saw Peter at the station. *(I saw Peter, but did not speak to him.)*

To be avoided are slang terms such as 'The party was only fun'.

Onomatopoeia

Onomatopoeia is the technical term applied to words which imitate the sounds they describe.

bang	buzz	coo	crash	flap	pop	quack	splash

In verse it is a device often used for effect.

Opinion

See: **In my opinion**

Opposites

By adding a prefix, the meaning of a word can sometimes be changed to the opposite.

a- :	amoral, apolitical
ab- :	abnormal, abuse
dis- :	disarrange, dissatisfy
il- :	illegal, illiterate
im- :	immovable, impolite
in- :	incapable, innumerable
ir- :	irregular, irresponsible
mis- :	misbehave, mis-spell
non- :	nonsense, nonaligned
un- :	unnecessary, unnatural

Words which end in the suffix '-ful' form their opposites by replacing the suffix with ' -less'.

careful - careless
harmful - harmless
useful - useless

See: **Antonyms**

201

Organization

Written material should be arranged in a systematic order of ideas, events and details. This is as true of an essay as it is of each paragraph of which it is composed.

1. Logical Order

There are various forms of organization which can be grouped together as those relying on logical order. Such arrangements are fundamental in the writing of expository prose and can be grouped as follows:

- Analysis: this refers to dividing a whole into its parts or indicating basic elements or internal divisions.

- Classification: in classification things are sorted into groups. Whereas in analysis the whole is divided up into its parts, classification draws similar things together to show what they have in common. By analysing a book you assess its contents, but when the book is classified it is put into a grouping with other books of the same kind.

- Comparison-contrast: by bringing out points of similarity (through comparison), or by emphasising differences (through contrast), or by combining these two procedures one is using comparison-contrast in order to arrange the material.
  One can do this in two ways:

  Discuss A fully; then discuss B fully; then discuss the similarities and differences.

  Discuss an aspect of A simultaneously with a corresponding one in B, indicating similarities or differences. Then move on to the next aspect.

2. Natural Order

There are two kinds of natural order.
- Time: when one writes a story or a narrative, one uses an

order of time to reflect the sequence or the chronological relationship of the points included. This is achieved by the use of words like first, then, eventually and finally.

- Space: in this approach, the elements and how they are related to each other in space are detailed; this arrangement is used to describe concrete objects such as a character's appearance, the description of a room, or a landscape.

See: **Essays; Instruction words**

-os, -oes

The spelling of the words 'potatoes' and 'tomatoes' causes some difficulty. Some words which were once abbreviations and some which are of foreign origin end in ' -os' in the plural forms.

curios	photos	dynamos	solos

See: **Spelling**

Ought

1. **Ought** expresses an obligation which is stronger than 'should'.

> You ought to study this afternoon.
> *(This statement implies that the studying is virtually a prerequisite, while **should** makes it less so.)*

2. **Ought** is used only in the present tense. To convey the past, the infinitive form is put into the past tense.

> I ought to leave now.
> I ought to have left yesterday.

See: **Anomalous finite verbs; Auxiliary verbs**

Overworked words

Try as far as possible in your writing not to use a particular word too frequently; if the direction of your argument demands the repetition of any concept use various synonyms.

See: **Clichés**

Owing to

See: **Due to**

P

Padding

Padding refers to the use of unnecessary words to 'fill out' a piece of writing. Unnecessary words are redundant words, and often detract from the writer's argument.

See: **Wordiness**

Paradox

A paradox is a statement which seems on the surface to be self-contradictory or absurd, but proves on examination to have validity.

More haste, less speed.

Paragraphs

There are three kinds of paragraphs in an essay: introductory, middle and concluding. Each of these has a specific function. The **introductory paragraph** contains the thesis statement, which gives the subject of the essay in a single sentence. The **middle paragraphs** each contain a topic sentence which develops a single fact or idea related to the thesis statement. The **concluding paragraph** draws the threads of the argument together, and attempts to show how, or to what extent the thesis statement in the first paragraph has been proved or addressed.

Some guidelines:

- Start a paragraph with an indentation.
- Ensure that each of the middle paragraphs expresses no more than one idea, and stick to it: do not introduce other ideas or topics.
- Never have only one sentence in a paragraph, as this indicates that the topic does not need a whole paragraph to itself.

See: **Essays; Topic sentences**

Parallel structures

If the structures within a sentence are not parallel there is the danger of **faulty parallelism**, which is the failure to use similar words to relate similar ideas.

> X I like studying, camping and to read.
>
> √ I like studying, camping and reading.

Paraphrase

1. To paraphrase is to put someone else's ideas in your own words while keeping more or less to the length of the original statement. (Thus it is different from making a précis, which summarizes and condenses the ideas.)

2. Paraphrasing is preferable to quoting unless a quotation is absolutely essential. The disruption in style which results from the insertion of quotations can be jarring to your reader.

3. In order to paraphrase, first read the passage carefully. Then put the text aside and try to put the same ideas in your own words. If the text is very complex, do this a sentence or two at a time. (If you are unable to do this, it probably means that you have not understood the text properly.) The other person's

ideas should be expressed in words and sentence structures which are your own, and you will only be able to do this if you have a complete and thorough understanding of the ideas.

4. A paraphrase should always be introduced by acknowledging the source.

> According to Rogers ...
> In Freud's view ...
> Ramaphosa is of the opinion that ...

5. Paraphrases should always be footnoted.

See **Footnotes; Plagiarism; Referencing**

Parenthesis (Parentheses)

See: **Brackets**

Participles

1. There are two kinds of participles: the **past participle** which usually ends in '-ed', '-d', '-t', '-en' or '-n'; and the **present participle** which always ends in '-ing'.

2. Participles are often used as adjectives or in participial phrases which qualify a noun.

> The **setting** sun cast a warm glow on the scene.
> Throw the **popped** balloon away.
> **Punched** black and blue, the **unmoving** man lay on the ground.

3. The **present participle**
   Present participles combine with the verb 'to be' to form the continuous (or progressive) tense of verbs.

> Women in the townships are organizing around issues such as
> the education crisis.
> I am waiting.

When '-ing' is added to a word which ends in a silent 'e', the
'e' is usually left out.

> glide - gliding   hide - hiding

When '-ing' is added to a stressed vowel and consonant, the
consonant doubles.

> sit - sitting   lap- lapping

4. The **past participle**

Past participles combine with auxiliary verbs to form perfect
tenses and the passive voice.

> He has **played** in the first team for years.
> Her views were **expressed** with conviction.

5. There are three uses of the participle which need to be
avoided.

- **Wrongly related participles**

> X **Playing** soccer in the park, a dog suddenly attacked me.
> *While the meaning is plain, the grammar of the sentence is*
> *weak: it is not clear whether the dog or the person is playing*
> *soccer.*
>
> √ While I was playing soccer in the park, a dog suddenly
> attacked me.

- **Unrelated participles**

> X **Standing** on the shore, the ship sailed past.
> √ While he was standing on the shore, the ship sailed past.

See: Dangling modifier

- **Fused participles**

This error often occurs because the proper gerund construction, which should be used with a possessive noun or pronoun, seems awkward. The solution is to reconstruct the sentence. Such sentences reveal that the gerund, which acts as a noun, is wrongly used as a participle.

> X I don't like you **taking** my things.
> √ I don't like your taking my things.
>
> X My mother disliked him **saying** that.
> √ My mother disliked his saying that.

See: Adjectives; Gerund

Parts of speech

Words can be divided into nine groups called 'parts of speech'.

- Nouns
- Adjectives
- Adverbs
- Verbs
- Prepositions
- Conjunctions
- Pronouns
- Interjections
- Determiners

A word is classified according to its function in a sentence, and the same word may be different parts of speech in different sentences.

(Consult the individual entries for each part of speech.)

Passed, past

1. **Passed** is used in verbal senses.

> We all passed the test.
> The ball was passed down the line.

2. **Past** is used in all other senses.

> She arrived at ten past two.
> Past exam papers are most valued.
> Two blocks past the park, turn left.

See: **Homonyms**

Passive voice

1. A verb is in the **active** voice if the subject of the sentence is the person or thing that performs the action described by the verb.

A verb is in the **passive** voice when the subject of the sentence is NOT the 'doer' or performer of the action described by the verb.

> Six blocks support the bridge.
> *This sentence tells us that the subject, blocks, is actively doing something to the object, bridge. The verb, support, is therefore in the active voice.*
>
> The bridge is supported by six blocks.
> *In this sentence, the verb, is supported, is in the passive voice as the subject, bridge, is passively supported by the six blocks.*

2. Try, wherever possible, to avoid passive constructions because they tend to be —

   • wordy (requiring more words than active constructions)
   • weak (the subject is acted upon, instead of acting)
   • vague (they sometimes omit the agent – that which is carrying out the action. In cases where the agent is omitted, the so-called 'Dummy Subject' is used.)

> It has been decided that ...
> It was discovered that ...
>
> *In these examples, the agent or 'doer' of the 'decision' and the 'discovery' is omitted and replaced with the Dummy Subject 'It'.*

3. Good writing contains active verbs, which keep it within a simple active pattern of subject-verb-object.

See: **Active, passive**

Percentage (percent)

It is quite acceptable to use the symbol % instead of the word 'percent' in our writing. However, using a numeral to start a sentence is not acceptable, so write 'Fifteen percent of the class ...' rather than '15% of the class ...'.

Person

Person	Singular	Plural	Reflexive
First person	I, me	we, us	myself, ourselves
Second person	you, your	you, your	yourself, yourselves
Third person	he, she, it	they	himself, herself, itself, themselves

211

Plagiarism

1. Plagiarism is a form of theft. It is the presentation of someone else's words, ideas, opinions, or facts as if they were your own. Plagiarism can easily be avoided by using footnotes to acknowledge all sources used.

2. Direct quotations (using the actual words of the original text) should be enclosed in quotation marks, and the exact source, including the page number, should be footnoted.

3. Paraphrases and summaries should be introduced by acknowledging the origin of the ideas (Freud states that ..., Mphahlele claims ...) and the sources should be indicated in a footnote.

4. Ideally, your writing should have as its core your own ideas. A paper which merely patches together quotations and paraphrases of other people's work is not worth writing, and certainly should not have your name appended to it.

5. Apart from your knowledge and ideas, and those of other writers, there is a body of common knowledge about every subject. This consists of facts, ideas, and theories which are so widespread and in such common use within the field that they are considered common property and as your rightful inheritance from the thinkers who have preceded you. General information known by most of the writers in a specific field can be considered to be 'common' and thus impossible to steal or plagiarize. If seven out of ten writers you read mention the same piece of information you can assume that it is common knowledge, and yours to use.

See: **Footnotes; Paraphrase; Quotations; Referencing**

Play

See: **Drama**

Plural forms

The general rule for making a plural form of a noun is to add
-s to the singular form. However, there are a number of words
which require different treatment.

1. Add **-es** for all those nouns ending in hissing sounds or
   sibilants.

ass - asses	box - boxes	buzz - buzzes
blush - blushes	latch - latches	gas - gases

2. Add **-es** for surnames ending in '-s'.

Barnes - Barneses
Soames - Soameses
Davis - Davises

3. Some nouns ending in '-f' or '-fe' follow the general rule.

chief - chiefs	hoof - hoofs	roof - roofs
cliff - cliffs	cuff - cuffs	scarf - scarfs
giraffe - giraffes		

4. Some nouns ending in ' -f', change the '-fe' into a '-v' and add
   -es in the plural.

knife - knives	life - lives
shelf - shelves	wife - wives

5. Where a noun ends with '-y' after a consonant, the '-y'
   disappears in the plural form and is replaced by **-ies**.

candy - candies	berry - berries

213

6. For a noun ending in '-y' after a vowel, the general rule applies.

> boy - boys
> valley - valleys

7. There is a small group of nouns for which the singular and plural forms are identical.

aircraft	cod	deer	forceps
grouse (bird)	salmon	sheep	swine

8. For most nouns ending in '-o' add **-es** in the plural form, but less familiar words, foreign derivatives, proper names and contractions of longer words follow the general rule.

	hero - heroes	potato - potatoes	negro - negroes
BUT	archipelagos	cameos	dynamos
	folios	ghettos	infernos
	manifestos	photos	pianos
	romeos.		

9. A few Latin words ending in '-um' have retained their Latin plural. However, in most cases, the tendency is to form the plural by applying the general rule.

	datum - data	stratum - strata
BUT	memorandum - memorandums	
	sanatorium - sanatoriums	
	spectrum - spectrums.	

10. Words ending in '-on' are increasingly treated according to the general rule.

> automaton - automatons
> BUT phenomenon - phenomena
> criterion - criteria

11. Most words ending in '-us' form the plural by adding **-es**, but a few retain the Latin plural.

> focus - focuses
> terminus - terminuses
> bonus - bonuses
> BUT stimulus - stimuli
> radius - radii

12. Some words ending in '-is' form the plural by ending in **-es**.

> analysis - analyses
> basis - bases
> crisis - crises
> oasis - oases
> axis - axes

13. Some nouns depart entirely from the usual forms. They are either survivors of Old English or words borrowed from other languages which have retained their foreign plural forms.

child - children	foot - feet
louse - lice	man - men
ox - oxen	penny - pence
tooth - teeth	bureau - bureaux
larva - larvae	libretto - libretti
plateau - plateaux	tableau - tableaux

14. Most compound nouns are made up of an adjective plus a

noun. The plural form of the noun is also used in a compound noun.

> gooseberry - gooseberries
> Englishman - Englishmen

15. When a compound noun comprises a noun plus an adjective or the equivalent of an adjective, the plural ending is used in the middle of the compound noun.

> court-martial – courts-martial
> looker-on – lookers-on
> son-in-law – sons-in-law
> mother-in-law – mothers-in-law

16. Where the word ends in '-ful', the plural ending has come to be added to the suffix.

> cupful - cupfuls
> handful - handfuls

17. The plural of Mr Buthelezi is Messrs Buthelezi while that of Miss Botha is the Misses Botha or the Miss Bothas.

Plural words

1. A number of words refer to items made up of two parts. They are plural words and require a plural verb.

braces	garters	goggles	knickers	pants
pincers	pliers	scissors	shears	shorts
suspenders	tights	trousers	tweezers	forceps

2. When one of these words is used with 'a pair of', the verb is in the singular.

> A good pair of scissors is an expensive item.
> An imported pair of shoes is a luxury item in one's wardrobe.

Point in time, at this

'At this point in time' is a barbarism that seems to have crept into the language to stay, but should be avoided by anyone wishing to write or speak with any measure of exactness. 'Now', and 'at this moment', are adequate substitutes.

> X At this point in time the new government is still finding its feet.
> X At this point in time I am studying Practical English.

See: **Wordiness**

Portray, portrait

Portray is a verb which means 'making a picture of something' or 'describing something vividly in words' or 'acting a particular part'.

Portrait is a noun which identifies 'a painting, drawing or photograph or a person' although it can also refer to 'a vivid description in words'.

The words are sometimes confused by those for whom English is not their home-language: the confusion is possibly the consequence of not sounding the last consonant,'t', in 'portrait' and thus mispronouncing the word.

Possessive case

A noun is used in the possessive case in order to show that the

217

individual or item mentioned is connected with something else.

> **Ntuli's** car needs a service.
> The hide **of a hippopotamus** is very thick.
> The **players'** boots were destroyed in the fire.

See: Apostrophe; Case; Genitive

Practice, practise

Practice is a noun.

> Doctors in private practice usually make more money than those in the civil service.
> Practice makes perfect.

Practise is a verb. As the participles **practised** and **practising** are formed from the verb, they too are spelt with an 's'.

> A good musician practises regularly.
> He is a practised liar.

*Just as **n** (for noun) comes before **v** (for verb) in the alphabet, so **c** comes before **s**.*
*Therefore the noun is spelt with a **c**, and the verb with an **s**.*

There is no distinction between the spelling of the noun and the verb in American English. Both are spelt **practice**.

See: Advice, advise; Licence, license

Précis

A précis is an abstract or summary which is intended to impart the vital elements of the original prose in a condensed form to someone who has not read the first version. The term précis is falling into disuse and is often replaced by the word summary. However, while a précis sets out to scale down the original, a summary may concentrate on a facet of the writing that is to be reduced.

Competence in the writing of a précis depends on practice. The editorials of newspapers provide readily available sources of suitable passage for practice in précis-writing.

Methods of writing a précis differ and the steps required will be reduced as the skill develops. A possible approach is the following.

1. Read the passage quickly so as to obtain the general idea.

2. Think of a good title for the passage, as this often helps to pinpoint the central concern.

3. Read through the passage slowly, marking or underlining the important points and connecting ideas.

4. Prepare a rough draft without looking at the original so as to ensure that your précis is written in your own words as far as possible. (This step may have to be left out if you are pressed for time.)

5. Read through the draft before writing the final version. Reduce it to the required length by substituting phrases for clauses, or words for phrases. Retain only the important points and leave out details, illustrations and examples.

6. Read over your précis to ensure that nothing important has been left out.The main points and the line of thought are important: the précis should therefore reflect the sequence of ideas and their connection. Above all, the précis must reveal that the original writing has been fully understood and no new matter should be introduced.

Predicate

In conventional grammar the predicate is the part of a sentence which expresses the state or actions of the subject plus any qualifications or modifications.

> They **participated in the carnival**.
> The dog **lay down on the mat to sleep**.

Prefer

When the past tense is used, the consonant 'r' is doubled: preferred.

See: **Consonants; Spelling**

Prefix

A prefix is a word element added to the beginning of a word to change the meaning. Prefixes are usually marked in the dictionary as 'pref.'.

Some common prefixes with their meanings are:

a-/ab- away	**ante-** before
anti- against	**bi-** two, twice
com-/con- with	**de-** down, away
dis- the reverse of	**ex-** out, remove
ex- former (always used with a hyphen, as in 'ex-president', 'ex-wife')	
in- in, on, onto, towards	**in-** negative (as in 'inconsiderate')
inter- among, between	**intra-** on the inside, within
mis- badly, wrongly	**multi-** many
non- not	**pan-** all
per- through, completely	**peri-** round, about
post- after	**pre-** before
pro- in front of, on behalf of, for	**re-** again, back

se- apart, without

trans- across, beyond

ultra- beyond

under- below

semi- half or part

tri- three

un- contrary to, not

up- upward

Prepositions

1. Prepositions are words such as 'at', 'in', 'with', 'by', and 'from'. A preposition is a word that marks the relationship between a noun or pronoun and another word.

> I found him **at** home.
> Put the food **in** the basket.
> He danced **with** every girl **in** the room.
> Lectures should start **on** time.

2. Certain verbs are always used with a particular preposition. The dictionary entry on any verb will usually give the prepositions with which it can be used.

> smile **at**
> remind **of**
> sorry **for**
> throw **at** / **to** (X throw with)
> explain **to**

3. There is an old rule which firmly enjoins one never to end a sentence with a preposition. Application of this rule can result in very awkward phrasing (as in 'This is something up with which I shall not put'), and thus should not be blindly used.

4. Prepositions are always followed by the object case of the pronoun.

> **to** whom   **with** him   **at** them

See: **Case**

Principal, principle

1. The word **principal** refers to a person and can best be remembered by its last letters ('pal' = person, friend). Principal means 'chief' and is used as either an adjective or a noun.

> The principal of the school is its most important (or principal) member.
> The principal character in the play is Macbeth.

2. The word **principle** means a 'fundamental or basic truth, or a guide to conduct'.

> He stuck to his religious principles and refused to gamble.

Programme, program

The use of **program** is common American usage. **Programme** is the spelling preferred in South African usage, although this is bound to change as the American influence becomes more pervasive. This is already evident in the field of usage related to computers, where **program** (for software) is the preferred spelling.

Pronouns

These words stand in for nouns and avoid boring repetitions of those nouns. When using pronouns, avoid errors or confusion by using the noun first, followed by the pronoun.

> When Sipho reached the station, he found that his train had already left.

There are several main kinds of pronouns:
- Personal pronouns
- Demonstrative pronouns
- Relative and interrogative pronouns
- Possessive pronouns
- Indefinite pronouns

1. Personal pronouns

The following words can be classified as personal pronouns:

First person pronouns	I / me	we / us	
	myself	ourselves	
Second person pronouns	you		
	yourself / yourselves		
Third person pronouns	he / him	she / her	they / them
	himself	herself	themselves
	one	it	
	oneself	itself	

In this category we include the personal pronouns which stand for those who are 'acting', those who are being addressed, and those to whom reference is made. Avoid the error of confusing the person, by mixing up pronouns such as 'he', 'she', 'you' or 'they' with 'one'.

> **I** was riding to town with **him** when **you** rode past with **her**.
> X **One** will make progress as long as **you** make enough effort.
> √ **One** will achieve if **one** tries hard enough.

The reflexive pronouns ('myself', 'yourself', 'himself', 'herself', 'oneself', 'itself', 'ourselves', 'yourselves' and 'themselves') also belong to the category of personal pronouns. These pronouns are called reflexive pronouns because they refer back to the subject of the sentence. They are often used for emphasis.

> **She** could imagine **herself** in that role.
> **I** found **myself** rejecting every suggestion.
> **He** paid for the ticket **himself**.
> **We** found the entrance to the cave **ourselves**.

See: **Self pronouns**

2. Demonstrative pronouns

Demonstrative pronouns point out something or someone.

this   that   these   those   such   the other   the same

> 'Which hat shall I wear?'
> 'You can wear **this** or **that**.'
>
> '**These** are the boys selected.'

3. Relative pronouns and interrogative pronouns

Relative pronouns are used for connecting or expressing a relationship.

who   whom   those   which   that

> The house **that** I saw had very small rooms.
> This ball **which** I bought yesterday has been punctured.
> People **who** exercise regularly enjoy better health than those **who** do not exercise.
> The boy to **whom** they gave the money lost it.

Interrogative pronouns are those used when asking a question.

who?   which?   what?   whom?   whose?

> **Which** design attracts you?   **Whose** shoes are brown?
> **Who** pays the full fare?   **What** are you doing tonight?

4. Possessive pronouns

Possessive pronouns are used to show ownership or possession.

mine   yours   hers   his   its   ours   theirs   whose

> The shoes are **mine**, the socks are **hers**.
> **Yours** is the house on the corner, **theirs** is the one next to it.

5. Indefinite pronouns

Indefinite pronouns refer broadly to unspecified numbers of people or things.

any   one   anyone   nobody   nothing   something

> **One** might expect something of that kind to provide interest.
> **Anybody** caught stealing must expect nothing but immediate arrest.

Pronunciation

Pronunciation is the way in which words are articulated. The English pronunciation of second-language speakers is usually influenced by their first language. Unless the pronunciation is so deviant that it is confusing to one's audience, a non-native accent is not a problem. The social stigma that used to be attached to non-native pronunciation is gradually becoming less of a factor as English becomes an international language with a number of variations in accent.

See: **Accent; Standard English**

Most of the larger dictionaries indicate a word's pronunciation by using a phonetic alphabet. It is worthwhile to become familiar with this and to use the dictionary whenever you are in doubt as to how to say a word.

Proofreading

This is perhaps one of the most important, yet most neglected aspects in the writing process. All work needs to be carefully read after the writing has ended – even professionals make unconscious errors, and these need to be set right before any piece of writing gets to the reader.

HINTS
- Wherever possible try to enlist the help of someone when checking your work: the 'objective' eye of an outsider will often spot mistakes before you do.
- Proofread line by line, and word by word: this will help you to find what is actually on the page instead of 'seeing' what you think should be there.
- Read aloud, rather than silently: often you will 'hear' an error before you see it.

Proportion

Proportion refers to a part of a total amount. Thus, if one concentrates on a particular section of an essay to the exclusion of other, equally important sections, the work will lack proportion.

Protagonist

A protagonist is the main character in a story or a drama. The word comes from the Greek *protos*, meaning 'first', and *agonistes*, meaning 'actor'.

Protocol

Protocol is the word which describes the expected code of behaviour on special occasions, or the expected forms of address used in formal written communications. The etiquette practised depends upon the formality of the event and the dignitaries involved. The protocols followed vary appropriately.

Much of this type of behaviour or practice is affected and is increasingly falling into disuse, but for those who wish to observe protocol the following guide to forms of formal address may be helpful.

Government, judicial and diplomatic titles in order of precedence, and appropriate forms of formal address:

1a. President

Envelope:	The President
Salutation:	Dear President
Ending:	Yours most respectfully
Invitation Card:	No card – letter to the President's Private Secretary
Speaking:	Mr President *and subsequently* President

1b. Wife of President

Envelope:	Mrs A Monghadi
Salutation:	Dear Mrs Monghadi *or* Dear Madam
Ending:	Yours most respectfully
Invitation Card:	No card – letter to the Private Secretary of the wife of the President
Speaking:	Mrs Monghadi/Madam

1c. President and wife

Envelope:	The President and Mrs A Monghadi
Salutation:	(Dear) Mr President and Mrs Monghadi
Ending:	Yours most respectfully
Invitation Card:	No card – letter to the President's Private Secretary
Speaking:	Mr President and Mrs Monghadi

2. **Executive Deputy**

Envelope:	The Executive Deputy President
Salutation:	Dear Deputy President
Ending:	Yours most respectfully
Invitation Card:	No card – letter to the Deputy President's Private Secretary
Speaking:	Mr Deputy President *and subsequently* Deputy President

3. **Chief Justice**

Envelope:	The Honourable B Ndumu, Chief Justice
Salutation:	Your Honour *or* (Dear) Mr Chief Justice (and Mrs Ndumu)
Ending:	Yours respectfully
Invitation Card:	The Honourable Mr Justice Ndumu (and Mrs Ndumu)
Speaking:	Mr Justice Ndumu, Judge, *or* Sir

4a. **Cabinet Ministers & Deputy Ministers**

Envelope:	(Mrs) A Pule, MP, Minister/Deputy Minister of ... *or* The Minister/Deputy Minister of ... (and Mr Pule)
Salutation:	(Dear) Madam/Mr Minister/Deputy Minister *or* Madam/Sir or Dear Minister/Deputy Minister
Ending:	Yours respectfully
Invitation Card:	(Mrs) A Pule, MP, Minister/Deputy Minister of... (and Mr Pule)
Speaking:	Madam/Mr Minister/Deputy Minister *or* Madam/Sir

4b. **Speaker of Parliament**

Envelope:	(Mrs) A Rangane, MP, Speaker Of Parliament
Salutation:	(Dear) Mr/Madam Speaker
Ending:	Yours respectfully
Invitation Card:	The Speaker of Parliament (and Mr Rangane)
Speaking:	Mr/Madam Speaker *then* Sir/Madam

4c. **Senator**

Envelope:	Senator R C Makgoba
Salutation:	(Dear) Senator *or* Sir/Madam
Ending:	Yours respectfully
Invitation Card:	Senator R C Makgoba (and Mrs Makgoba)
Speaking:	Senator *then* Sir/Madam

5. **Ambassador**

Envelope:	His Excellency the Ambassador Extraordinary and Plenipotentiary of ... *or* His Excellency (Mr) J Komane Ambassador Extraordinary and Plenipotentiary of ... *or* Their Excellencies the Ambassador Extraordinary and Plenipotentiary of ... and Mrs P Komane
Salutation:	Your Excellency *or* Mr Ambassador *or* Dear Mr Ambassador *or* Your Excellencies
Ending:	Yours respectfully
Invitation Card:	His Excellency the Ambassador of ... *or* Their Excellencies the Ambassador of ... and Mrs P Komane.
Speaking:	Mr Ambassador *or* Your Excellency

6. **Provincial Premier**

Envelope:	Mr T Sekekane, Premier of ...
Salutation:	Dear Mr Premier *or* Dear Mr Sekekane
Ending:	Yours respectfully
Invitation Card:	The Premier of ... (and Mrs Q Sekekane)
Speaking:	Mr Premier *and then* Sir

7. **Judge**

Envelope:	The Honourable Mr Justice F Mpofu
Salutation:	Your Honour *or* Dear Judge (and Mrs Mpofu)
Ending:	Yours respectfully
Invitation Card:	The Honourable Mr Justice F Mpofu (and Mrs O Mpofu)
Speaking:	Mr Justice Mpofu, Judge, *or* Sir *and in court* Your Honour *or* M'Lord

229

8. **Member of the Executive Committee of the Provincial Legislature**

Envelope:	Mr M Tau, Minister of ...
Salutation:	Dear Mr Tau *or* Sir
Ending:	Yours respectfully
Invitation Card:	Mr M Tau, Minister of ... (and Mrs Tau)
Speaking:	Mr Tau *or* Sir/Madam

9. **Member of Parliament**

Envelope:	Mr B Botile MP *or* B Botile, MP
Salutation:	Dear Mr Tau *or* Sir
Ending:	Yours respectfully
Invitation Card:	Mr M Tau, Minister of ... (and Mrs Tau)
Speaking:	Mr Tau *or* Sir/Madam

10. **Mayor**

Envelope:	His Worship the Mayor of ... *or* Her Worship the Mayoress, Councillor G Ndlovu
Salutation:	Mr/Madam Mayor/ess *or* Dear Mr/Mrs Ndlovu
Ending:	Yours respectfully
Invitation Card:	His/Her Worship the Mayor/ess of ... *or* His/Her Worship the Mayor/ess, Councillor G Ndlovu (and Mr/Mrs Ndlovu)
Speaking:	Mr/Madam Mayor *and then* Sir/Madam *or* Alderman *or* Councillor

Religious titles and forms of formal address:

1. **Archbishop**

Envelope:	His Grace the Lord Archbishop of ...
Salutation:	Your Grace
Ending:	Yours faithfully
Invitation Card:	His Grace the Lord Archbishop of ... , Dr H E Saintly
Speaking:	Your Grace

2. **Bishop**

Envelope:	The Right Reverend the Lord Bishop of ...
Salutation:	My Lord
Ending:	Yours faithfully
Invitation Card:	The Right Reverend the Lord Bishop of ... , Mr B Holy
Speaking:	Your Grace

3. **Member of the clergy**

Envelope:	The Rev. O Soul
Salutation:	Sir
Ending:	Yours faithfully
Invitation Card:	The Rev. O Soul
Speaking:	Reverend *or* Sir *or* Mr Soul

See: **Letter writing; Salutation**

Proverbs

Proverbs are short, pithy sayings. They are those words of ordinary people that have come to be accepted as wise and sensible. They are part of the language and are used on suitable occasions to express an idea better than a speaker can. They often reflect unchanging human nature. They are generally found to be inappropriate in formal, academic writing.

> A change is as good as a holiday.
> There is more to it than meets the eye.
> It is like water off a duck's back.
> The child is father of the man.

See: **Clichés**

Public speaking

The attention span of the average adult has been found to be

12 minutes, when a single mode of communication is used. Public speakers who are aware of this fact – or intuitively understand how to communicate well with an audience – will deliberately build variations into their approach whenever the subject matter, or the occasion, demands a longer speech.

Speakers who place great store on making excellent speeches often spend an hour in preparation for each minute they intend speaking. This is not always possible but thorough preparation is necessary both for your own sake and out of respect for your audience.

Experience is the best teacher of what works when speaking in public. However, the following points may be useful guidelines:

• Prepare

1. Decide on the important and specific points you wish to share.
2. Pick the main idea or theme of your presentation and make all the other points subordinate to it.
3. Seek for a provocative title that points to what you are going to say and focus on that theme, so that your audience knows what you are talking about.
4. Research your subject to add facts and backing to your own experience.

• Build an outline

1. Introduction: Find a startling opening statement; then state your main idea, weaving in some local interest peculiar to the audience's experience to get them on your side.
2. Body of the speech: Develop each of the points that support your main theme, illustrating them with anecdotes and stories drawn generously from your own experience. Slant your material to match your audience's interests and focus.
3. Conclusion: Build to the climax; summarize your key points before finally stating your main idea again; then stop.

• **Master the content**

1. Write down your main points as notes – or in full if you feel very nervous about the event.
2. Go over the speech often enough to become familiar with the contents, but do not memorize the wording.
3. Revise those sections that need more interesting material by adding suitable anecdotes.
4. Check the speaking arrangements to make sure that all your effort is not in vain.

• **Deliver the speech**

1. Speak naturally. Do not adopt a preacher's style. Use strong, simple language.
2. Be animated in voice, expression and attitude. Move as needed but avoid mannerisms.
3. Do not worry about being nervous. Almost all speakers are nervous regardless of how often they have spoken in public.
4. Look individual members of your audience in the eye. Do not focus on one place in the room. Speak to all of your audience.
5. Keep control by dealing with distractions immediately and effectively.
6. Do not read your speech. Use your notes if you need to, but try to do so sparingly.
7. Observe the time limit you have been given, both for the sake of your audience and for others who may be sharing the platform with you.

Punctuation

Punctuation is a collection of marks, each with highly specialized functions, used to mark off written texts into meaningful readable units.

The most common marks of punctuation are:
• the full-stop .
• the comma ,
• the semi-colon ;

- the colon :
- the question mark ?
- the exclamation mark !
- quotation marks " " or ' '
- the apostrophe '
- the dash –
- parentheses ( )
- ellipsis ...
- brackets [ ]

See the separate entries for each individual punctuation mark.

Pursue, persuade

The confusion over these words is a peculiarly South African phenomenon.

Pursue means to 'go after in order to catch up with someone or something'. In its noun form, the word is **pursuit** or the act of **pursuing**.

To **persuade** someone, on the other hand, means 'to convince' that person of the point at issue.

	We pursued the idea of driving to Harare in convoy, but then decided that it would be unnecessary.
	The concept that every woman is in pursuit of a man to marry is a sexist stereotype.
BUT	We persuaded him to accompany us to the theatre.
	Subtle persuasion is an art mastered by all advertising copywriters.

Question mark (?)

1. The question mark is used at the end of a direct question.

> What time is it?
> How can one believe him?

2. Question marks are also used at the end of statements which are indirect questions.

> You don't expect me to take you seriously?
> It's surely not lunchtime already?

3. Question marks are placed inside quotation marks if they belong to the quotation. Question marks are placed outside quotation marks if the quotation is not a question, but the whole statement is.

> The lecturer said, 'Why haven't you prepared the work?'
>
> Why did he say, 'You are a fool' ?

Questions

1. In English, questions are made by putting the auxiliary verb in front of the subject.

> △ You (have) paid the telephone account.
>
> Have you paid the telephone account?

2. When there is no auxiliary verb, the question is made by inserting the auxiliary verb 'do'.

> You like chocolate.
> Do you like chocolate?

3. When a **question word** is used (who, when, where, what, how, why) it is usually placed at the head of the question, and the auxiliary verb is put before the subject.

> △ You (are) laughing.
>
> Are you laughing?
> Why are you laughing?

4. In spoken English, statements spoken with a rising intonation are questions.

> You're sure you want to come?

5. **Tag-questions** are statements with a question at the end made up of an auxiliary verb and a personal pronoun. A tag question is more a request for confirmation (Is this true? Do you agree with me?) rather than a request for information.

> She's very clever, **isn't she**?
> He's not coming, **is he**?

Positive statements are given negative tags, and negative statements are given positive tags. A positive statement with a positive tag is used to express sarcasm or scepticism.

Oh, so Nomsa's sick, **is she**?
(This implies that one thinks that Nomsa is not really sick, but is making an excuse.)

Nomsa's sick, **isn't she**?
(This is merely a request for confirmation. It does not imply any scepticism about Nomsa's illness.)

6. In reported questions, normal word order is retained and the auxiliary is not moved.

'When will you be finished?'
He asked when you would be finished.

'Are you going home then?'
He asked if you are going home then.

Notice that if there is no question word in the direct question, 'if' or 'whether' is used in the reported question.

Question whether

Whether is used in reported speech to introduce a question that does not have a question word.

'Will you accompany me?'
He asked whether you would accompany him.

We discussed whether we should start divorce proceedings.

See: **Indirect speech; Questions**

Quicker

Quicker is often used incorrectly as an adverb. The correct form is **quickly**.

> He did the job more quickly *(that is, faster)* than I could have.

Quiet, quite

Often needlessly confused, these words have quite distinct meanings.

> Please be quiet; I am trying to concentrate.
> I have been working on this for quite some time.

Quotation marks

Quotation marks, also called inverted commas (either double " ", or single ' '), have the following uses.

1. Double or single quotation marks are used to enclose a direct quotation, or the actual words of a speaker.

> "Voetsak!" he yelled.
> 'To be, or not to be' is perhaps Hamlet's most famous line.

2. Quotation marks are used to mark out words which are being discussed as words, or used in an unusual way.

> To refer to a woman as a 'chick' is not only over-colloquial, but also sexist.
> 'Overweight' is a politer term than 'fat'.

3. Quotation marks are used for the titles of short stories, paintings, songs, and poems, but not for the titles of books.

> Simon and Garfunkel's 'Bridge over Troubled Water' was voted number 1 in Radio 702's 1988 listener survey of the one hundred most memorable songs.
>
> "Lamb to the Slaughter" is perhaps Roald Dahl's most satisfying short story.

4. For a quotation enclosed within a quotation, use single quotation marks if the main quotation used double quotation marks, and vice versa.

> "Can you believe it?" asked Marie. "He actually had the cheek to say 'I have had better macaroni cheese before, but this is passable'!"
>
> When the director said, 'Let's start again on the line "Romeo, Romeo, Wherefore art thou Romeo?", and let's have some real emotion this time', there were groans of exhaustion from Juliet.

Other punctuation marks are used with quotation marks as follows.

5. Commas and full-stops can be placed inside quotation marks.

> 'If you are in a hurry,' she said, 'I can do it immediately.'

6. If the quotation is a question, the question mark goes inside the quotation marks. If the whole sentence is a question, but the quotation is not, the question mark goes outside the quotation marks. The same rule applies to exclamation marks.

> Did he really call her 'a cast-iron crumpet'?
> His question was, "What are the real facts here?"

7. Semi-colons and colons almost never occur at the end of a quotation, so they are always placed outside the quotation marks.

> He said, 'Of course you can trust me'; but I was not convinced.

8. A dash is placed inside the quotation marks if it represents an interruption in the speaker's words.

> 'But I don't want –' she began, and then threw her hands up in frustration.

9. Doubles or singles?
Different institutions have different styles, some preferring double quotation marks, and some insisting on single.

The argument for using single quotation marks in all cases, reserving double quotation marks only for quotations within quotations, is based on the 'cleaner' appearance of a typed page, which looks less 'fly-specked' when single quotation marks are used.

No one convention is the right one, but once one has been chosen it must be used consistently throughout.

Quotations

When to quote:

1. Quote sparingly. An article or paper which quotes frequently will have a discordant style.

2. Quote when using a well-known quotation. One would not want to re-word 'To be, or not to be', for example.

3. Quote when someone else's words are the most effective and concise way of presenting an idea. Direct quotes are

sometimes essential evidence in convincing your reader.

How to quote:

1. Short quotations should be meaningfully and grammatically incorporated into your sentence. Do not merely tack them on to your text.

2. Use quotation marks for short quotations.

3. Long quotations should be -
   • indented
   • blocked off from your text
   • single-spaced, marked off from the rest of your text by a double-space at the beginning and at the end
   • without quotation marks.

4. One or two lines of poetry may be included in your text, enclosed in quotation marks, with the line division marked by a slash (/). Longer quotations must be blocked and centred.

5. Omissions from a quotation should be marked with an ellipsis (...).

See: **Ellipsis**

6. If you need to insert a word into a quotation, or change a word in order to link the quotation sensibly with your sentence, the word should be enclosed in brackets.

See: **Brackets**

7. Always acknowledge the source of your quotation.

See: **Footnotes; Plagiarism; Quotation marks; Referencing**

R

Racist language

Racist language is the use of terms which reflect and encourage stereotyped and prejudiced thinking about the issue of race. A particularly thorny problem in South Africa, this has to be approached and written about with as much objectivity as possible in order to avoid causing offence, or creating the impression of biased and murky thinking in one's writing. Terms such as 'black', 'white' and 'coloured' (or the more politically correct term, 'so-called coloured') should not be capitalized, and may be used within quotation marks if one wishes to emphasize their imprecision and/or their loaded connotations.

Usage of the terms as if they were nouns ('the Blacks', 'the Whites' and so on) is also generally found offensive. 'Europeans', used to refer the 'white' population group in South Africa, is not only outdated, but also inaccurate. It should not be necessary to point out that denigrating terms for any racial group have no place in any type of writing or other communication.

Just as the use of expressions such as 'a woman doctor' and 'career woman' are regarded as sexist, so the deliberate indication of race (usually in phrases such as 'a black writer' or 'a black manager') is seen as racist. The implication in these cases is that 'male' or 'white' are the norm, and that 'deviations' from this norm (female, black) have to be indicated explicitly. This implication both conveys and encourages stereotyped and prejudiced thinking, and such usage should therefore be avoided.

See: **Sexist language**

Raise, rise

The verb **raise** is transitive and must have an object.

> The man raised the revolver, took aim and fired.

The verb **rise** is intransitive and is literal in meaning.

> I rise early on work-days
> The cost of living rises rapidly.
> The level of water in the dam rises after each storm.

By contrast, the word **arise** has metaphorical meaning.

> A doubt arises in my mind when you look away.
> When such a situation arises few know what to do.
> Questions arise when people are unsure of their position.

Rather ... than

Rather ... than are correlative conjunctions which balance two parallel structures. The two structures thus balanced should be the same (two adjectives, two nouns, two pronouns, two clauses, and so on).

> I would call her clever rather than brilliant
>   (adj)   (adj)
>
> It ought to have been Mosa rather than Patricia who got the prize.
>   (noun)   (noun)

> I prefer to sleep rather than to party.
>   (infinitive)   (infinitive)
> I would rather be your friend than be your lover.
>   (phrase)   (phrase)

Re

The word **re** means 'about'. It is half of the Latin phrase *in re* and is used in legal language as well as in clichéd business letters, as a heading, to refer to the points contained in those letters. It can usually safely be omitted from such subject headings.

Realism

Realism is a way of representing life in art and literature. While romantic art presents life as we would like it to be, realism attempts to depict life as accurately as possible, in the way in which it really is. Realism tends to focus on the average, the commonplace, and the mundane, not only in its subject matter, but also in its style.

See: **Classicism; Romanticism**

Reflexive and relative pronouns

See: **Pronouns**

Referencing

One of the most important characteristics of academic writing is that it acknowledges its sources. There is a vast treasure house of knowledge written about, dreamt up, and pondered over by other scholars. This treasure house is yours to share, provided you observe the courtesy of recognizing that you are using other people's words and ideas. Referencing is important, firstly, as academic good manners – a form of thanks, if you like, to those scholars whose writing and thinking has helped to shape yours. Secondly, people reading your writing might want to read some of your sources for themselves. An idea or quotation that you use might inspire them to set upon a new track of discovery, and they may want to go back to one or more of your original sources. So referencing is also important as a gesture of generosity to your readers.

Complete referencing has two components: the acknowledgement of the source of a quotation or idea within the body of your essay or article, and a section at the end of your essay or article (Works Cited or Bibliography) which lists all the sources you have consulted and referred to.

The rules are as follows:
1. In the body of your text –
   name of the author, year of publication of the text, and the page number of the quotation or reference
2. In the bibliography –
   Books: name of author, year of publication, title (underlined or in italics), place of publication, publisher
   Articles: name of author, year of publication, title of article (in quotation marks), title of journal (underlined or in italics), journal volume number, pages

---

Entries in your text:

> 'Elephants are not easily house-trained' (Van Zyl, 1993:125)

> 'There are a number of disadvantages to keeping elephants as pets: size of accommodation needed, house-training, and volume of food consumed being but a few' (Van Zyl, 1991: 34).

OR   Van Zyl suggests that there are difficulties inherent in house-training elephants (Van Zyl,.1991; 1993).

> Entries in the bibliography:
>> Van Zyl, D.A. 1991. *Keeping Unusual Pets*. Cape Town: Oxford University Press.
>> Van Zyl, D. A. 1993. 'The Pachyderm as Pet: A Re-assessment.' *Journal of Pet Care*, 6, 29-46.

3. If you have used two or more sources by Van Zyl, the dates will tell your reader which one is the origin of your quotation (eg Van Zyl, 1985; Van Zyl, 1987). You should list the sources chronologically in your bibliography. If Van Zyl has published two or more works in the same year, you need to add lower case letters (a, b, c ...) to the date in order to differentiate between them.

> Van Zyl, D. A. 1994a. *Care and Feeding of Elephants*. Johannesburg: HarperCollins.
> Van Zyl, D.A. 1994b. 'Socio-economic variables affecting elephant care: A longitudinal study.' *Pachyderm Quarterly* 37(2), 134-156.

4. For articles or chapters in books edited by someone else, you would cite the author of the article as indicated above. In your bibliography, you will provide an entry for the individual article or chapter, and an entry for the book or volume from which the article/chapter was taken.

> Entry in your text:
>> A number of researchers have investigated the problem of providing elephants with adequate exercise (Van Zyl, 1995; Bengu, 1995).

Entries in the bibliography:
> Bengu, S. M. 1995. 'Exercise requirements of large mammals.' In Mesthrie, 1995: 58-72.
> Mesthrie, R. ed. 1995. *Practical Pet Management*. Johannesburg: Prentice-Hall.
> Van Zyl, D. A. 1995. 'The relationship between fitness levels and contentment indices in pets.' In Mesthrie, 1995: 129-145.

5. Citing Electronic Sources

Increasingly, more and more information is being found in electronic format. Quotations and ideas gleaned from these need to be acknowledged. The entry in the text is similar to that used for paper-based references (except that you will not have a page number to cite). The bibliography format is as follows:

Author's last name, First name. 'Title of Work.' Title of Complete Work. (if appropriate) [protocol and address or path] date of message or visit.

Entry in your text:
> Hodges (1995), a writing theorist, refers to 'our field's sense of secondary citizenship in English departments'.

Entry in your bibliography:
> Hodges, Elizabeth. 1995. 'Re: Compositionists as writers.' WPA-L@asuvm.inre.asu.edu (21 November 1995).

The electronic world of information changes extremely rapidly, and it is wise to ensure that you keep up to date with new conventions. The following WWW sites offer updated information on citation style:

APA and MLA Citation Styles
http://www.utexas.edu/depts/uwc/.html/citation.html

Citation Style for Internet Sources by Mark Wainwright
http://www.cl.cam.ac.uk/users/maw13/citation.html

CyberCitations
http://www.mbnet.mb.ca/~mstimson

MLA-Style Citations of Electronic Sources by Janice Walker
http://www.cas.usf.edu/english/walker/mla.html

How do you cite URL's in a Bibliography?
by Jeff Beckleheimer
http://www.nrlssc.navy.mil/meta/bibliography.html

University of Tennessee, School of Information Science
http://cobweb.utcc.utk.edu/~hoemann/style.html

Hawaii's Online Learning Assistance
http://kalama.doe.hawaii.edu/hern95/pt035/

The Alliance for Computers and Writing
http://prairie_island.ttu.edu/acw/acw.html

6. On e-mail, you will not have access to underlining or italics.
   The current convention is to insert a short underline before
   and after the title of a work you cite (eg _WordPower_).

See: **Footnotes; Paraphrase; Plagiarism; Quotations; Quotation marks**

Register

Register refers to the level of formality in one's writing or
speech. One's language should be appropriate in tone, style,
and word choice. Its appropriateness depends on one's
audience, the context, and the purpose of one's
communication. A formal register is inappropriate in a friendly
letter, while an informal register is equally out of place in a

report or article. Generally, all written communication in an academic or business environment should have a formal register, and in this type of communication one should adhere to all the formal rules of expression contained in this book. In conversation and in personal writing, an informal or colloquial register is perfectly acceptable.

See: **Audience**

Relation, relative

In the context of relationships, these two words are synonyms. They both mean a kinsman or kinswoman, or one who is related by blood or marriage.

> He is no relation/relative of mine.
> However, she is my relation/relative.

Repetition

Needless repetition of words, ideas and sentence patterns diminishes the effectiveness of writing. Thus, try not to use any word or description too often, vary the length of sentences, and find different ways of expressing an idea that is repeated.

Reported speech

See: **Indirect speech; Questions**

Respectively

Respectively, meaning 'to refer to persons or things in the order in which they are mentioned', should not be confused with 'respectfully'.

> Zodwa, Khombe and Fatima came first, second and third,
> respectively.
>
> (Zodwa came first, Khombe second, and Fatima third.)

Revision

Writing is a process and one of the most important steps in that process is revision. Once the piece of writing has been drafted completely in rough, it should be carefully revised. This means that you should view what you have written critically. Look at your writing from the point of view of unity, coherence and emphasis.

Unity is achieved by defining the main topic and deciding what ideas are relevant to that topic. Less important ideas must receive the correct amount of emphasis and not be given more prominence than the main idea.

Coherence is attained by arranging the ideas in a proper or logical order or sequence, while the grammatical use of the language is vital to the coherence of any writing.

You may find that using the checklists below will help you.

Revision Checklist

1. Does each paragraph have a topic sentence or main idea?
2. Does each paragraph have at least one sentence in addition to the topic sentence? (ie Does each main idea have at least one supporting idea? Are there examples and supporting details included in each paragraph?)
3. Does the topic sentence of your introductory paragraph make a general statement about the content of your essay?
4. Are the topic sentences of the rest of your paragraphs related to the subject of your essay, as indicated in your introductory paragraph?
5. Do two or more paragraphs have the same topic sentence?

6. Do the topic sentences of the paragraphs follow in logical sequence to each other?
7. Does the topic sentence of your concluding paragraph sum up the main argument of your draft, as expressed in the topic sentences of the preceding paragraphs?
8. Have you written the passage with your specific audience in mind?

Editing Checklist

1. Have you punctuated the passage correctly?
2. Have you avoided the use of jargon?
3. Have you eliminated colloquialisms or slang?
4. Have you checked the spelling of words you are unsure about?
5. Have you used simple English words?
6. Are your sentences short and clear?
7. Have you avoided the use of abbreviations?
8. Have you replaced any words or expressions used too often?
9. Have you cut out unnecessary adjectives and adverbs?
10. When you read through the writing aloud does is 'sound' right?

As the final steps in revising your writing, re-write the passage and check that all the changes you have made have been included. Lastly, read out the final product aloud once more to assess its fluency and correctness.

Rhetoric

Rhetoric was originally defined by Aristotle as the art of 'discovering all the available means of persuasion in any given case'. Classical rhetoricians focused on oral discourse, but rhetoric has come to mean the art of composing in general. Texts in rhetoric discuss issues such as 'invention' (the generating of material, finding arguments and proofs), 'disposition' (the arrangement and organization of material), and style.

251

Rhyme

Rhyme is based on matching sounds.

1. **Full rhyme** is the matching of the sounds of two words. The matching portions consist of the last stressed vowel of each word and any succeeding consonants or unstressed syllables.

2. **Partial rhyme** (also called 'imperfect', 'near' or 'slant' rhyme) is an imperfect matching of two words. The stressed vowels may be only approximate or quite different, while the consonants following the stressed vowels are similar or identical.

3. **End rhyme** is the most common form of rhyme. This is the rhyme that occurs at the ends of verse lines. A rhyme scheme is the pattern made by the end rhymes in a poem, identified by successive letters of the alphabet.

4. **Internal rhymes** are rhymes which occur within the verse line.

Because I'm Black	
Because I'm black	a
You think I lack	a
The talents, feelings and ambitions	b
That others have:	c
You do not think I crave positions	b
That others crave.	c
Because the people eat and sing	d
And mate,	e
You do not see their suffering.	d
You rate	e
Them fools	f
And tools	f
Of those with power and boastful show;	g
Not Fate, but fault, has made things so.	g

> Beware! these people, struggling, hold   h
> The last trump card;   i
> Subdue them now you may   j
> 'Tis but delay. Another day   j
> When God commands they will be bold ...   h
> They will strike hard!   i
>
> H I E Dhlomo

Rhymes such as 'black - lack' are called **masculine rhymes** because they consist of single stressed syllables.

Rhymes such as 'ambitions - positions' are called **feminine or double rhymes** because there is a match between both stressed and unstressed syllables.

'Have - crave' (lines 4 and 6) is a **half-rhyme**.

'Delay - day' (line 18) is an **internal rhyme**.

Rhyme provides aural satisfaction, and creates a pleasing aesthetic effect in the patterns it produces, but in literary criticism it is important to concentrate on rhyme primarily to the extent to which it reinforces and contributes to meaning.

See: **Metre**

Rhythm

Rhythm is the flow of sound which results from the stress variations of spoken language. In prose, the stresses fall irregularly, while in verse there is a regular rhythm or pattern to the stresses.

See: **Metre**

Romanticism

The Romantic Period in literature spans the years from the outbreak of the French Revolution in 1789 to approximately 1830.

Writing classified as 'Romantic' is characterized by emphasis on –
* the importance of the writer's own feelings and inner emotional world;
* the world of nature;
* an optimistic view of humankind's potential and aspirations
* a dissatisfaction with inherited rules and imposed restrictions on creative enterprise.

See: **Classicism; Realism**

S

Salutation

Salutation is the term used to describe a sign or greeting expressed in recognition of the arrival of another person or when communication with someone else is commencing. It is used especially to describe how the text of a letter begins.

Salutation	Associated Ending
Dear Sir	Yours faithfully
Dear Madam	Yours faithfully
Dear Ms Lorien	Yours sincerely
Dear Mr Jabulani	Yours sincerely
Dear Dr Motlana	Yours sincerely
Dear Prof Ramaphele	Yours sincerely

See: **Letter writing, Protocol**

Same, similar

Sometimes these words are confused. **Same** means that two things are identical. **Similar** means that there is a resemblance between two items.

The word **same** is also used in a clumsy, old-fashioned way instead of the pronouns 'it' or 'this' in some business letters.

> X We acknowledge receipt of the parcel. Same will be returned in a fortnight.

255

Sarcasm

Sarcasm is a form of irony, in that it signifies a remark that is the opposite of what it appears to mean. However, unlike irony, sarcasm is often intended to hurt someone's feelings.

> 'Running over the cat was really a clever idea', she said nastily.

See: **Irony; Satire**

Satire

Speech or writing which uses irony, sarcasm or ridicule so as to show up or discourage stupidity or evil is called satire. Satire sets out to teach.

See: **Irony; Sarcasm**

Scarcely

Scarcely has a somewhat negative meaning. The word means 'hardly', 'very little' or 'with difficulty'.

> I have scarcely any time left.
> I could scarcely reach the top of the steep hill during the Comrades Marathon.
> She had scarcely any money left after her visit to the casino.

Scotch, Scots, Scottish

Scotch is used as an adjective in 'Scotch whisky' and 'Scotch tweeds'. It is also commonly used alone as a noun meaning 'whisky'.
Scottish is the more formally correct adjective to refer to the nation, the countryside, and Scotland's institutions and characteristics.

Scots can be a noun (the language spoken, the people) and is used as a adjective only in established expressions, such as regimental names (the Scots Guards).

Self pronouns

Sometimes these pronouns are referred to in this way, but they are essentially personal pronouns. The words referred to are:

myself	ourselves	yourself	yourselves	himself
herself	itself	themselves	oneself	

See: **Pronouns**

Semi-colon (;)

This form of punctuation is used between elements that are similar in idea or construction. It marks off a longer pause than a comma, and can be used to link two ideas in a sentence.

> In Zimbabwe there are more than six thousand dairy farmers; despite this, the Cooperative Union seems to devote most of its attention to the 360 timber growers.

Sentences

A sentence is the complete expression of a thought or idea so that it makes total sense to the reader or hearer; it begins with a capital letter and ends with a full-stop. There are three forms of the sentence:

- statements (The door has been opened.)
- questions (Has the door been opened?)
- commands (Open the door.)

Every sentence has a subject and a predicate, with a simple

257

sentence making a single statement about the subject and a compound sentence making two or more statements about the subject.

> Subject: The farmer
> Predicate: looked at the cows in the kraal.

See: **Predicate**

A sentence can also have an object, which is dependent on the verb. This means that if there is no verb there can be no sentence. Instead, the construction will be either a phrase (a group of words without a subject or a verb) or a clause (which is not a complete sentence, and cannot stand by itself).

> Sentence: We stood in the shade of an overhanging rock.
> Phrase: of an overhanging rock
>
> Sentence: He fell ill, so that his project was not completed.
> Clause: so that his project was not completed

Sexist language

Sexist language is language that conveys stereotyped and biased views of the human race, and of the role of women in society, through linguistic means such as use of the words 'man' or 'mankind', 'he' as the generic pronoun, and condescending nomenclature to refer to women.

The language we use interdependently reflects and affects our perception, and thus the issue of gender in writing is an important one. Research has indicated, for example, that the use of the terms 'man' and 'mankind' to a statistically significant degree evokes images of men only. It has also been clearly indicated that 'man' in the sense of 'male' so overshadows 'man' in the sense of 'human being' as to make the latter use both inaccurate and misleading for purposes both of conceptualizing and communicating.

Good writers or speakers cannot ignore the effect they have on their audience, and it is undeniable that current audiences have an increasingly sophisticated ear for sexist under- and overtones. Just as there is no longer any justification for perpetuating racist stereotypes and bias in one's use of language, so sexist usage is increasingly being regarded as indicative of lack of education or extreme subjectivity on the part of the speaker or writer.

Guidelines

There is little point in substituting one stereotype with another. A grimly determined replacement of every 'he' with a 'she' has a shock value that is of assistance if one is trying to make an ideological statement, but one should rather aim for a natural combination of both pronouns. The main point is not to be reduced to counting incidences of each pronoun, but to convey, through one's choices of language, an awareness that roughly half the world's population is female, and that roles and expectations are no longer rigidly defined by gender. (There is no justification, for example, for constantly referring to doctors as 'he'.)

The pronoun 'one' offers an alternative to the gender-marked pronouns, and there is also the option of omitting pronoun reference at all.

X If a student is unable to complete the course he may apply for a refund.

√ A student who is unable to complete the course may apply for a refund.

Use of the plural ('people', 'writers', 'students', 'politicians') allows one to use 'they' – perhaps one of the most successful and least ambiguous ways of dealing with the issue of the gender of the population one is writing for and about.

While pronouns are one of the most obvious manifestations of sexist bias in one's language, the term 'man' is an equally thorny problem. There are instances where its elimination creates ludicrous effects (a 'personhole' instead of a 'manhole', for example), which essentially trivialize the issue. However, substitution of 'people' or 'human beings', or fairly simple re-wording ('working hours' instead of 'man-hours'; 'staffed' instead of 'manned', for example) are relatively painless ways of removing possible causes of offence or inaccuracy.

Another source of sexism in language is the use of terms to refer to women. 'Girls' and 'ladies' are generally found unacceptable as terms to refer to women, and condescending, patronizing and/or demeaning nomenclature should be avoided. (If 'career-man' is tautological, then 'career-women' is equally so, and if a new male member of staff is never referred to as 'a bubbly blond who is father to three children as well as being career-orientated', then neither should female staff members be thus defined.) Also, tacking an '-ess' ending onto a common gender English word is reasonably resented by most people thus defined. ('Poet', for example, is the preferred term, regardless of the gender of the person identified.)

Many libraries have a range of reference works with guidelines for gender-neutral language use (for example Rosalie Maggio's *The Nonsexist Word Finder: A Dictionary of Gender-free Usage*) and Unisa Press offers a manual called *Beyond the He-Man Approach*, available in all eleven official languages.

See: **Gender; Racist language**

Shades of meaning

These are the different interpretations that can be derived from a piece of writing, and often depend on the emphasis given to a particular aspect by the writer.

See: **Feeling in words; Synonyms**

Shall, will

1. **Shall** and **will** are auxiliary verbs used to express future tense. **Shall** is used for the first person (singular and plural), and **will** is used for the second and third persons (singular and plural).

> I shall go.   We shall go.
> You will go.   You will go.
> He, she, it will go.   They will go.

2. **Shall** can also be used for an order or obligation (in the sense of 'must').

> Thou shalt not steal.
> He shall not be allowed to write out any more cheques until he has cleared his overdraft.

3. **Will** is used with the first person to express determination or resolve.

> I will finish this work today, come what may.

Should of

See: **Contractions**

Similar, like

The adjective **similar** means 'having a striking resemblance or likeness'. **Like** is the word used more often and serves as a preposition.

> My car is like yours.
> He has an ungainly gait. He runs like a camel.

Similar is usually used with 'to'.

> My car is similar to yours.

See: **Like, as; Same, similar**

Simile

A **simile** is a figure of speech which explicitly compares two things, using the word 'like', 'so', or 'as'. (It thus differs from a metaphor where the comparison is implicit.)

> As cold waters to a thirsty soul, so is good news from a far country.
> Proverbs 25:25
>
> ... the evening is spread out against the sky like a patient etherized upon a table ...
> T S Eliot

> Harlem
>
> What happens to a dream deferred?
>
> Does it dry up
> like a raisin in the sun?
> Or fester like a sore –
> And then run?
>
> Does it stink like rotten meat?
> Or crust and sugar over –
> like a syrupy sweet?
>
> Maybe it just sags
> like a heavy load.
>
> Or does it explode?
>
> Langston Hughes

This poem operates on five similes. A dream deferred is like a raisin, a festering sore, rotten meat, a sweet, and a heavy load. The final statement lacks the word 'like' and is therefore an implied metaphor, comparing a deferred dream to a bomb.

See: **Analogy; Metaphor**

Simplicity

The best sentence is usually the simplest and, often, the shortest.

See: **Wordiness**

Singular or plural

The real subject of a sentence determines whether the verb is singular or plural.

> About one in ten doctors does house-calls these days.
>
> *'Does' is correct because the subject is the singular 'one'. There is an understandable tendency to write 'do' because of the nearness of the verb to 'ten doctors'.*
>
> One of those children who believe in magic tries to copy the trick.
>
> *Here 'tries' is in the singular because its subject is 'one'. 'Believe' takes the plural form because 'who' refers to the plural subject 'children'.*

See: **Agreement; Collective nouns; Plural forms; Plural words**

Slang

Slang is more appropriate to spoken than to written English, and is not used in formal situations. Slang thus falls into the same category as colloquialisms. It is often difficult to distinguish between the two as today's colloquialism often comes from yesterday's slang. Slang is usually indicated in the dictionary by the abbreviation *sl*.

See: **Audience; Register**

Small, little

1. **Small** is used to talk about size. It is the opposite of 'big' or 'large'.

> She is such a small girl, one can hardly believe that she is at high school already.

2. **Little** is used to talk about size which evokes some emotion in us – either affection, distaste, amusement, or irritation.

> 'Oh, what a sweet little boy!'
> He's a nasty little man.
> Look at the funny little monkey.

3. In describing objects, **small** is used to refer to size, while **little** refers to quantity.

> I'd like a small coffee, please. *(ie a small cup)*
> I'd like a little coffee, please. *(ie only about 100ml of liquid)*

4. **Small** and **little** used together make your language sound affected.

> X She's a small little girl.

Soliloquy

Playwrights (notably Shakespeare) sometimes make use of

this dramatic device to reveal the thoughts and feelings of a particular character to the audience. Often the speech is uttered as an aside, and the other persons on the stage are meant to show no awareness of it.

Somebody

The following usage is well known though seldom heard:

> He is nobody in town but he is a somebody in his office.

In South African townships, **somebody** is commonly used in the place of nouns such as 'person' or 'individual'.

> X She is an important somebody in that church.

Sort of

Meaning 'somewhat', 'in a way' or 'rather', **sort of** is a vague expression that should be avoided in formal English – and especially in writing. Another expression which falls into this category is 'kind of' ('He was feeling kind of lazy').

South Africa

This is a proper noun, often used as an abbreviation of Union of South Africa or Republic of South Africa. Note that no hyphen is used between the two words.

South Africanisms

There are many loan words and other terms drawn from other languages that have become characteristic of English in South Africa. These forms of expression can be called South Africanisms.

> to go farming/teaching *(to become a farmer/teacher – origin unknown)*
>
> hold thumbs *(keep one's fingers crossed – from the Afrikaans 'duim vashou')*
>
> go garshly *(proceed carefully – from the Nguni 'hamba kahle')*
>
> soul tiffy *(an army chaplain in the Technical Services Corps – an abbreviation of the British army term for mechanics: 'artificer')*
>
> Ja well no fine
>
> finish and klaar
>
> to pack out one's suitcase *(instead of 'unpack'; translated from the Afrikaans 'uitpak')*

See: **Foreign words**

Spelling

Language is essentially speech and the alphabet is a means of representing speech on paper. English is difficult to spell because its written forms are inconsistent, unreasonable and impossible to reduce to absolute rules. There are several reasons for this. The sounds of a language are always slowly changing. We use a pronunciation different from that of our grandparents. English is a hybrid language which has gathered words from many sources and continues to do so. Some of these borrowed words take on an English form of spelling, others look foreign but are given an English pronunciation, and yet others keep both their foreign spelling and pronunciation.

To complicate matters for South Africans our practice is to use the British forms of spelling. We nevertheless read a good deal that makes use of American spelling which has influenced some aspects of British spelling.

266

British	American
foetus	fetus
enquiry	inquiry
armour	armor
colour	color
odour	odor
centre	center
theatre	theater
mould	mold
plough	plow
levelled	leveled
travelled	traveled
programme	program

Why struggle with spelling? The answer is simple. Consider the following two sentences and decide which is the better.

Teechers shoed stop there pupills from useing the meny larj wirds.

The tendency towards verbosity which pertains in the character of aspirant scholars should be eliminated by the studied endeavour of their teachers.

At first glance, the second sentence seems the better one. Actually the first sentence is the better one because it is more direct and simple. But the spelling mistakes make it difficult for us to take it seriously. Mis-spelling distracts the reader.

Reading is good for spelling. The more you read, the more you will get to know certain spelling patterns.

Good spellers use a dictionary to find the correct spelling for words about which they are doubtful. They also use their basic senses when they study the spelling of a difficult word.

- Eyes – they look at the word and note its syllables
- Ears – they say the word aloud so as to hear it in use

- Touch – they write the word out more than once so as to feel its shape

They compose a sentence, using the word, so as to imprint its meaning in use in their memories.

In South Africa words are often mis-spelled because they are badly pronounced. The following examples of mispronounced words will help you overcome this source of spelling error.

> athlete not 'athelete'
> probably not 'probly'
> library not 'libry'
> February not 'Febury'
> mathematics not 'mathmatics'
> surprise not 'suprise'
> could have not 'could of'

A word of caution: pronunciation is far from an infallible guide to correct spelling. The last syllables of the following words have the same pronunciation, but they are all spelled differently: writer, beggar, mediocre, doctor.

Spelling rules

To eliminate some of the difficulties of English spelling, learn the following rules. They apply often enough to be useful.

1. I before E
   Remember this rule by the jingle:

   > Write I before E
   > Except after C,
   > Unless sounded like A
   > As in neighbour or weigh.

i before e	ei after c	ei sounded like a
belief	ceiling	weigh
thief	perceive	reign
pierce	deceive	veil
yield	receive	counterfeit
relieve		
EXCEPTIONS: leisure	financier	seize

2. Drop the silent E
   When a suffix beginning with a vowel is added to the word ending in a silent 'e', drop the 'e'.

```
please + -ure = pleasure
admire + -able = admirable
ride + -ing = riding
create + -ive = creative
dilate + -ion = dilation

EXCEPTIONS: dyeing, noticeable, advantageous.
```

When a suffix beginning with a consonant is added to a word ending in a silent 'e', keep the 'e'.

The silent 'e' is often kept after 'c' or 'g' to make sure that the sound remains soft.

```
sure + -ly = surely
advertise + -ment = advertisement
like + -ness = likeness
care + -ful = careful

EXCEPTIONS: wholly, truly, awful, fifth, twelfth.
```

3. Change Y to I
   Unless the suffix begins with 'i', change 'y' to 'i' before a suffix.

> baby + -es = babies
> carry + -ing = carrying (suffix begins with an 'i')
> defy + -ance = defiance
> forty + -eth = fortieth
> busy + -er = busier
>
> EXCEPTIONS: dryness, shyness, slyly.

4. Double a final single consonant before a suffix beginning with a vowel.

> hop + -ed = hopped
> slip + -ing = slipping
> pot + -er = potter
>
> EXCEPTIONS: buses, gases.

5. Double the final consonant of a word ending with an accented last syllable.

> admit + -ed = admitted
> occur + -ed = occurred
> forget + -ing = forgetting
>
> EXCEPTIONS:
> benefit + -ed = benefited ('t' is preceded by 'i' but does not end the accented syllable)
> appeal + -ed = appealed ('l' is preceded by two vowels)

6. Do not double the final consonant if the word ends with two consonants.

```
stitch + -ed = stitched
last + -ing = lasting
toast + -er = toaster
```

7. Nouns which end in a sound that can be easily joined with -S usually form their plurals by adding -S.

book	books
tree	trees
bean	beans
ache	aches
flower	flowers
picture	pictures

8. Nouns which end in -O, that have long been in use in English, end in -OES in the plural form.

buffalo	buffaloes
cargo	cargoes
echo	echoes
mosquito	mosquitoes
potato	potatoes
tomato	tomatoes
volcano	volcanoes
zero	zeroes

Nouns that end in '-o', that were originally abbreviations, before they came to exist as words in their own right, end in '-os' in their plural forms.

curio	curios
photo	photos
radio	radios

Nouns borrowed from other languages often also end in '-os' in their plural forms.

commando	commandos
dynamo	dynamos
stiletto	stilettos
studio	studios

9. Nouns ending in a vowel plus -Y take only an -S in their plural forms

alloy	alloys
boy	boys
chimney	chimneys
display	displays
monkey	monkeys
valley	valleys

Verbs ending in the same way form the third person singular by adding an -S.

plays	enjoys	buys

10. Plural nouns borrowed from French, Greek and Latin often retain the plural form of the original language

alumnus	alumni
analysis	analyses
crisis	crises
datum	data
phenomenon	phenomena

Accepted practice is to anglicize the plural form wherever this is appropriate.

Singular	Foreign plural	Plural in use
focus	foci	focuses
index	indices	indexes
memorandum	memoranda	memorandums
radius	radii	radiuses
stadium	stadia	stadiums

See: **Plural forms**

11. Words that end with a silent -E drop the -E when -Y is added to form an adjective. When an adverb is formed, -LY replaces the -E or the -LE for words that end in those forms

ice	icy
stone	stony
gentle	gently
due	duly
fashionable	fashionably

12. Words ending in -C add a -K with the addition of the suffixes: -ED, -Y, -ING, -ER

frolic + -ing = frolicking
panic + -er = panicker
picnic + -ing = picnicking

13. Words ending in a silent -E drop the -E when joined with a suffix beginning with a vowel, but retain the -E when joined with a suffix beginning with a consonant

WORD	+ -ING	+ -ED	+ -FUL
hope	hoping	hoped	hopeful
grace	gracing	graced	graceful

273

14. Most words that end in -F, change the -F to -V and add -ES in their plural forms. However, some of the words ending in -F merely add an -S in the plural form.

	calf - calves	shelf - shelves
	knife - knives	wife - wives
BUT	hoof - hoofs/hooves	
	scarf - scarfs/scarves	
	staff - staffs/staves	

REMEMBER: IN ENGLISH, THERE ARE MANY EXCEPTIONS TO RULES AND IN SOME INSTANCES CONVENTION, RATHER THAN LOGIC, APPLIES

Split infinitive

In 1986, Style magazine gave Archbishop Desmond Tutu the Style Award for Getting Priories Right in the Face of Adversity, for the following comment:

'I reckon that what I'm doing is, to follow a biblical paradigm, to constantly be speaking ... oh, I've split an infinitive (bursts into uncontrollable laughter) ... I'll have to change that. I can't stand split infinitives.'

Archbishop Desmond Tutu to a television crew interviewing him at a mass funeral for unrest victims.

An infinitive is the basic form of the verb, preceded by 'to'.

to understand
to eat
to think
to talk
to argue

See: **Infinitive**

An infinitive is **split** when any words intrude between 'to' and the verb. A common feature, particularly in journalism, the split infinitive evokes in language purists a horror similar to that of a vegetarian faced with steak tartare. In Latin, the infinitive marker is attached to the word (*amare:* to love) and the feeling is that even though the 'to' is a separate word in the English infinitive, the infinitive remains a single syntactic unit which should not be split.

The issue of split infinitives is, however, a subjective and ideological one to a certain extent. Tolerance levels in English teachers vary, some seeing the rule as outdated and pedantic, and others refusing to allow any split infinitives at all. A fairly general trend seems to be that split infinitives are tolerated more easily in informal writing than in formal writing.

The following split infinitives are likely to be tolerated:
He seemed determined **to really enjoy** himself.
I'd like **to really understand** Nietzsche.
The object is **to further cement** trade relations.
The detective said it is difficult **to always catch** your man.
For Germany **to repeatedly invade** Western Europe was inexcusable.

The following sentences are generally found unacceptable:
X He began **to slowly get up** off the floor.
X The pupils were told **to quickly put** their books away.
X I plan **to eagerly grasp** the opportunity.

The trend seems to be that an adverb that is acting more as an intensifier (such as 'really') is not as jarring as an adverb of manner (such as 'eagerly') which carries a heavier load of meaning, and is as a result more intrusive, seeming almost to 'rupture' the infinitive.

As with many grammatical issues, the question of the split

infinitive is one that is subject to change under the influence of colloquial usage. A fair rule of thumb at present is to avoid split infinitives as far as possible in formal writing, keeping in mind that to deliberately avoid a split infinitive is to sometimes write unnatural English.

Standard English

This term is used to refer to the sort of English that is purported to be spoken formally by educated people in Great Britain and the Commonwealth countries. It is the kind of English that gives little indication of a speaker's origin and is sometimes defined as BBC English or Received Pronunciation. For the better part of the 20th century it was the ambition of educated people in the United Kingdom to acquire this manner of speaking and it was the form that foreigners aspired to learn. The written form of Standard English is more conventional, accurate and logical than the spoken version.

Standard English aims at uniformity of vocabulary and syntax that fits within the norms of traditional grammar. The advantage is that understanding is facilitated. The risk is that language loses its vitality because, when it is standardized in its written form, language is judged by its correctness and not its relevance and succinctness. Permitting the rules of the written language to predominate deprives the language of its dynamic richness and flexibility. However, good correct English serves a social need by ensuring that universal communication is made possible. The important point is that the rules of syntax must not be rigidly applied or else the invigorating value of dialects, slang, popular speech and colloquialisms will be lost.

Perhaps fortunately, the standardization of modern English is not as complete as the pedants would have it. Trends such as the popularization of local dialects in the United Kingdom have emphasized the vigorous enrichment of English by users of the language. Scholars cultivate and refine such language so as to ensure accurate and unambiguous communication. A legitimate pursuit is perhaps to strive for purity, but only as far as this is feasible without any loss of scope, subtlety or vigour in English usage.

In South Africa tension exists between those on the one hand who advocate striving to permit only Standard English to be taught and used formally, and, on the other hand, those who believe that the development of a unique South African English should be encouraged. This clash of view has been acute and most evident as national language policies, in the pursuit of equity rather than language equality for the country's eleven official languages, have been developed.

The fear of those who call for adherence to Standard English norms in the written form is based on the belief that a local variety of English may depart so much from its parent language that not only its precision and range will be lost, but South African English may even cease to be understood by English speakers in other countries. This fear ignores the reality of the universal means of communication that have been ushered in by the electronic age. The consequent and growing dependence on common technology and the strong global desire to preserve English as a lingua franca, as well as the extent to which English is already the educational and commercial language of choice in South Africa, make it improbable that South African English will evolve at such variance from its root form.

The debate is complex, but echoes 19th century arguments that American and British forms of English were destined to become incomprehensible to each other within a century. This has not happened and now appears improbable.

277

Stanza

A stanza is a grouping of the lines of a poem. A stanza may be marked by a recurrent rhyme scheme, and often is made up of lines of uniform length and metre.

See: **Metre; Rhyme**

Style

The word 'style' refers to the way in which a message is expressed. Style cannot be satisfactorily explained or defined. Nor is there a set way in which to develop style.

Style is influenced by three factors:
- the content of the message;
- the individual or people to whom the message is addressed;
- the occasion, or the publication in which the message is to be communicated.

The approach to style that should be followed is that advocated by W Strunk and EB White in *The Elements of Style*: write with plainness, simplicity, orderliness and sincerity.

Style evolves from within, but the application of the following set of **guidelines** will help to achieve pleasing and effective forms of composition.

1. Focus on the message and play down the part of the writer.

2. Write naturally. Do not try to adopt an assumed form of expression.

3. Write with a plan.

4. Write plainly and simply by not using descriptive words that are unnecessary.

5. Describe accurately. Any excess will detract from the message, as will the qualification of statements by the use of words such

as 'very', 'pretty', 'some', 'little' or 'rather'. Use ordinary words – not multi-syllabic words – and use language that will be understood.

6. Keep a tight rein on the contents. Do not ramble or digress.

7. Make a point once. Avoid repetition.

8. Identify the speaker when writing dialogue and do not use dialect unless you have an ear for it.

9. Write clearly, but do not be so brief that necessary details are left out.

10. Stick to facts and limit points of opinion.

11. Use figures of speech sparingly.

12. Write in English – do not show off your knowledge of other languages.

13. Ensure correct spelling. Use a good dictionary.

14. Revise and rewrite until the final product seems to be concise, clear, sincere and correct.

See: **Affectation; Business writing; Clichés; Clumsy expression; Register; Slang; Wordiness**

Subject

The subject of a sentence is the noun used for the person or thing doing what is described by the verb.

The bird flew swiftly.

The banana ripens on the tree.

The girls smiled.

Iqbal and I were the first to arrive.

Magenthrie and she win whenever they play as a pair.

In the last two examples, the subject of each sentence comprises more than one item. The form of the verb must therefore be plural.

See: **Organization**

279

Subordination

Where the main clause states the main argument in a sentence, the **subordinate clause** gives the secondary element. There are various guidelines for putting subordination into practice.

1. Relative pronouns – that, which.
   Relative pronouns can in some cases be understood – ie they are omitted in the actual sentence, but understood to be there.

> The computer, **which** had been of such use, finally stopped working.
>
> The notes [that] he made were incorporated in the essay.

2. Subordinating conjunctions – that, although, if, because, until, where, as if, since, so that

> He failed the examinations **because** he did not study.

3. Adverbs – when

> After the holiday, **when** he went back to work, he discovered that he had not really had any rest.

4. Participles – verbs acting as adjectives

> **Having been accused** of neglecting his work, he decided to look for another job.

Use subordination carefully. Beware of dangling modifiers!

See: **Dangling modifiers**

Such as

Such as is used to qualify a word by offering examples. Place it next to the word it is qualifying.

> The shop stocks a range of goods, such as groceries, electrical appliances and furniture.
>
> World class players, such as English internationals, play in the Italian soccer league.

Suffixes

Suffixes are endings added on to words to change their meaning or their grammatical function. They can be used to form –

• Nouns showing which agent is responsible for an action.

> cap**tain**   engin**eer**   dent**ist**   stud**ent**   shep**herd**   mission**ary**

• Abstract nouns

> patron**age**   critic**ism**   friend**ship**   tra**dition**   good**ness**

• Diminutives

> drop**let**   pupp**y**   duck**ling**   part**icle**

• Adjectives

> laugh**able**   hope**ful**   act**ive**   use**less**   god**like**   love**ly**

- Adverbs

> head**long** sad**ly** for**ward** back**wards** side**ways**

- Verbs

> educ**ate** length**en** low**er** modi**fy** adver**tise**

See: **Prefixes**

Summaries

While there is little difference between a summary and a précis, a distinction can be made. A **précis** is a shortened version of the entire original. A **summary** is usually an abbreviated version of an aspect or part of the original. For example, the evidence supporting only one side of an argument might be summarized.

See: **Précis**

Syllable

1. A syllable is a word or part of a word containing one vowel sound. Consonants may precede and/or follow the vowel. Words with one vowel sound form a single syllable, and the consonants on either side of the vowel belong to that syllable.

> at   on   black   thin   ring

2. A vowel sound forms the nucleus of the syllable. Words with two vowel sounds have two syllables, words with three vowel sounds have three syllables, and so on.

> pardon – par/don   examination – ex / am / i / na / tion

3. Certain consonant groups cannot begin a word or syllable in English. You would never (in English) find a word beginning with 'nd-', 'rd-' or 'ng-', and so a syllable would not start with these either.

   Thus, you could not possibly syllabify 'ponder' as 'po/nder', or 'hanger' as 'ha/nger', or 'pardon' as 'pa/rdon'.

4. Syllables are important in hyphenating words at the end of a line. You should always break a word at the end of a syllable. One-syllable words can thus not be hyphenated.

See: **Hyphen**

Symbols

A symbol is a sign or mark representing something else. It is a form of shorthand and is used to represent an idea, person or thing. Examples are the Cross, which stands for Christianity, the ZCC star, or the Star of David standing for Judaism. Some words have symbolic connotations: 'gold' usually signifies 'wealth'; a 'dove' is a symbol of 'peace'. Symbols often have emotional significance: the Russian communist hammer and sickle symbol evokes feelings of patriotism for citizens of the Soviet Union, or feelings of antipathy in citizens of those countries opposed to communism.

Synonyms

Synonyms are words which have similar or the same **denotative meaning**. (The denotation of a word is its literal, dictionary meaning.)

```
abolish / exterminate
adventure / escapade
odour / smell
```

Very few words, however, have identical **connotations** (the attitudes, feelings and images evoked by the word). While 'fat', 'plump', 'overweight', and 'obese' are synonyms, they convey quite different attitudes and feelings. 'Plump' is a far more flattering term than 'fat', for example. Similarly, words like 'odour', 'smell', 'stench', and 'fragrance', while synonymous, have very different connotations.

See: **Feeling in words**

Writers often use synonyms to avoid over-using one word. In consulting a thesaurus, however, you should be careful to choose a synonym that not only shares denotation with the word you want to replace, but also shares most of the connotations.

Syntax

Syntax refers to the correct arrangement of words in the sentence.

See: **Sentences**

T

-t, -ed

Some words have past participle and past tense forms which
end either in **-ed** or in **-t**, whereas the **-ed** form is standard for
most verbs.

Verb	Standard -ed past participle	Alternative -t form of past participle
burn	burned	burnt
dream	dreamed	dreamt
kneel	kneeled	knelt
lean	leaned	leant
spell	spelled	spelt
spill	spilled	spilt
spoil	spoiled	spoilt

See: **-ed, -t; Participles; Verbs**

Teach

See: **Learn**

Technical terms

See: **Jargon**

Tense

Tense is the system that shows time. Tensed verbs create a
sequence of time frames within each sentence, and between
sentences.

Tenses are formed either by changing the verb, or by adding auxiliary verbs. Tenses can be Present, Past, or Future. Individual entries follow for each of these, in alphabetical order.

See: **Verbs**

Tenses, Future

1. Simple Future Tense

FORM

will/shall + base form
OR
am/are/is + going to + base form.

SINGULAR	PLURAL
I shall work	We shall work
I am going to work	We are going to work
You will work	You will work
You are going to work	You are going to work
He/she/it will work	They will work
He/she/it is going to work	They are going to work

The simple future tense is used –
• to express future time
• to make a prediction
• to express intention

> Once you start working here, you **are going to work** harder than you ever have before.

2. Future Progressive

FORM

will/shall + be + -ing form

SINGULAR	PLURAL
I shall be working	we shall be working
you will be working	you will be working
he/she/it will be working	they will be working

The future progressive tense is used –
• to say that an action will be in progress at the particular moment in the future

> Don't interrupt me for the next few hours, **I'll be taking** a nap.

3. Future Perfect Tense

FORM

will/shall + have + past participle

SINGULAR	PLURAL
I shall have worked	we shall have worked
you will have worked	you will have worked
he/she/it will have worked	they will have worked

The future perfect tense is used –
• to say that something will have been completed by a certain time in the future.

> They **will have finished** their meeting by lunchtime.

287

4. Future Perfect Progressive

FORM

will/shall + have been + -ing form

SINGULAR	PLURAL
I shall have been working	we shall have been working
you will have been working	you will have been working
he/she/it will have been working	they will have been working

The future perfect progressive tense is used –
* to describe a continuous action occurring up to and including a certain time in the future.

By next October, **I shall have been working** here for four years.

See: **Shall, will**

Tenses, Present

1. Simple present

FORM

base form of verb + -s ending for third person singular.

SINGULAR	PLURAL
I work	we work
you work	you work
he/she/it works	they work

The simple present tense is used –
* to indicate present time
* to indicate habitual action or general truths

> 'Botha **lines** up the ball. He **kicks** ... it**'s** a mighty kick ... it**'s** over!
> The crowd **is** on its feet! Northern Transvaal **wins**!'
>
> I **live** in Johannesburg.
> I **go** to gym twice a week.
> I **see** my mother every Christmas
> Water **boils** at 100°C.

2. Present Progressive Tense

FORM

am/are/is + verb + -ing

SINGULAR	PLURAL
I am working	we are working
you are working	you are working
he/she/it is working	they are working

The present progressive tense is used –
- to refer to actions that are going on at the moment of speaking
- to describe a continuous action

> Children! Please don't shout while I **am speaking** on the
> telephone!

3. Present Perfect Tense

FORM

have/has + past participle

SINGULAR	PLURAL
I have worked	we have worked
you have worked	you have worked
he/she/it has worked	they have worked

The present perfect tense is used –
* to indicate an action beginning in the past but completed now in the present. The past event has a present importance.

> A bomb **has exploded** in a Pretoria shopping centre.
> The President **has been assassinated**.

Tenses, Past

1. Simple Past Tense

FORM

past tense form of verb

SINGULAR	PLURAL
I worked	we worked
you worked	you worked
he/she/it worked	they worked

The simple past tense is used –
* to refer to a completed event in the past

> I **worked** as a secretary for three years, now I am a trainee personnel officer.

2. Past Progressive Tense

FORM

was/were + -ing form

SINGULAR	PLURAL
I was working	we were working
you were working	you were working
he/she/it was working	they were working

The past progressive tense is used –
* to refer to a continuous action in the past which was happening at a particular past moment.

> I **was having** breakfast when my lift arrived.
> I **was working** while you **were playing** golf.

3. Past Perfect Tense

FORM

had + past participle

SINGULAR	PLURAL
I had worked	we had worked
you had worked	you had worked
he/she/it had worked	they had worked

The past perfect tense is used to –
* indicate an event in the past time which ended when another event, now also past, occurred. Past perfect thus refers to a 'second' or earlier past.

> I told him that he **had been** very unprofessional in his behaviour.
> Although she knew that she **had met** him before, she could not remember his name.

4. Past Perfect Progressive tense

FORM

had been + -ing form

SINGULAR	PLURAL
I had been working	we had been working
you had been working	you had been working
he/she/it had been working	they had been working

The past perfect progressive tense is used to–
* talk about continuous actions or situations which had been going on up to the past moment that we are referring to.

> I had been gossiping about her when she came into the room.

See: **Verbs**

Terrible

Terrible is an overworked word. Strictly, it means 'causing great fear or horror'. Terrible is often misused in forms such as 'It was terribly nice of her'. Here the word is used as a synonym for 'very', although the words are not comparable.

See: **Misused words**

Terrific

Terrific is used to describe something which causes terror. The word has come to have an overworked, colloquial meaning of 'very great or extreme'.

> X We had a terrific time at the amusement park.

See: **Misused words**

Than

Than is correctly used after a comparative adjective or adverb.

> Her cloths are cleaner than yours.
> Sand-filters clean the water better than other filters.

Than is incorrectly used when it is linked to the words listed below. The words are given with their correct combination words.

prefer **to**   different **from**

Thank you

Thank you should always be written as two words.

The

The definite article, **the**, points to a specific person or thing.

> The donga has been effectively repaired

See: Articles

Their, there

Their means 'belonging to them'.
There has a number of meanings, all of which make it completely different from 'their'.

> This is their house.
>
> She lives not far from there.
> There is the pen I want.
> Please don't go there.

Theme

A theme is the predominant idea in a piece of writing. It is different from the plot or story in that the latter is a series of events, while the theme is the linking idea or message behind the events.

For example, the plot of William Golding's *Lord of the Flies* concerns a group of boys marooned on an island. They become steadily more and more savage, kill each other and lose all remnants of civilization. The theme is that humankind is inherently evil and, given an absence of civilized restraints, this evil will predominate.

Themselves

Themselves is the pronoun used when people or animals are the objects of their own actions. (There is no such word as 'themself': **themselves** is always used in the plural.)

> The children treated themselves to an ice-cream.
> They blamed themselves for causing the fire.

See: **Case; Pronouns; Self pronouns**

Therefore, therefor

Therefore is an adverb which means 'for that reason'.
Therefor is an archaic word which means 'for that object or purpose' and is usually used in place of the object of a sentence. Note the difference in spelling and use.

> Sibongile was tired. She therefore went to bed early.
>
> How much is the book? The price is R12 therefor.

Thesis

A **thesis**, also called a dissertation, is a lengthy piece of original written work or research, presented by a student to earn a Master's degree, or a Doctorate.

The word 'thesis' means a proposition, and a written thesis usually examines or defends a proposition in the field of study chosen by the student.

This

See: **Demonstratives; Pronouns**

Titles

1. Titles of books
   These should be underlined (in printed works, the titles of books are italicized).

2. Titles of poems, essays, stories or sections
   The title of any part of a longer work (such as a book) should be placed in quotation marks.

> Please study the section entitled 'Rhythm in Prose and Poetry', which you will find in GH Vallins' *The Best English*.

See: **Referencing**

3. Titles of people

See: **Abbreviations; Mr, Mrs, Miss, Ms; Protocol**

Topic sentences

A **topic sentence** presents the main idea of a paragraph. Each paragraph should be unified and deal with a single idea, which can be summarized in a single sentence – the topic sentence. Everything else in a paragraph is designed to explain or expand upon the idea contained in the topic sentence.

A topic sentence is often placed early in a paragraph, as the first or second sentence, so that the reader knows from the beginning what the paragraph is about. Sometimes a topic sentence is held back to the end of the paragraph so that the main point gains emphasis, or in order to provide evidence, which will make the idea contained in the topic sentence more acceptable to the reader. A topic sentence may, however, be stated both early on and restated – in different words – at the end, as an emphatic summary of the main point.

Occasionally a topic sentence is implied, not stated, by the way in which all the presented details support one central idea.

A good topic sentence emphasizes the subject of a paragraph and explains the main idea about the subject – it stresses the focus of the paragraph.

---

1. Travelling is a wonderful experience.
[This topic sentence has a broad subject, travelling. It has a vague focus – 'wonderful experience'.]

2. Travelling overseas provides a range of new experiences and insights into the way of life of other people.
[The subject, travelling overseas, narrows attention to a specific area of exploration. The topic sentence also focuses more sharply on the nature of the results of travel. It is consequently a better topic sentence than the first example.]

3. Independent overseas travelling enables one to visit those places one wishes to see, and one can tarry or move on in personal response to the experiences of different places and people.
[In this topic sentence, the subject is narrowed further to independent overseas travelling. The focus also sharpens to reflect personal interests and reactions to the experiences.]

In paragraphs of exposition (explanation) and argument the topic sentence is usually explicitly stated. In paragraphs of narration (story-telling) and description the topic sentence is often only implied, but it should still be clearly communicated to the reader. For this to happen, the writer must keep the topic sentence in mind when writing, and must not break the principle of unity by introducing a new topic or view at the end of a paragraph.

See: **Paragraphs**

To, too, two

These three words are pronounced almost identically but have very different meanings and functions.

To is often either a preposition pointing in the direction of something, or a particle joined with the infinitive form of a verb.

See: **Infinitive**

Too is either an adverb meaning 'also' or an adverb of degree modifying adjectives or adverbs.

Two is a noun or adjective referring to the number 2.

> He caught the train **to** Durban. (preposition)
> The book is easy **to** understand. (particle)
>
> I have been to Cape Town **too**. (also)
> This dress is **too** small for me. (adverb of degree)
>
> **Two** can play at a time.
> Cut the apple into **two** pieces.

Toyi-toyi

The liberation struggles in Zimbabwe, Namibia and South Africa introduced this noun into English in southern Africa. It is used to describe the rhythmic chanting or shouting of slogans and singing of protest songs, while groups of demonstrators or protesters are performing a high-stepping militant dance and shuffle in unison. A **toyi-toyi** can happen in one place or while moving slowly and relentlessly forwards. It has an inspirational effect on the participants and evokes a sense of solidarity and defiance even when faced with possible forceful intervention.

The origins of the word are obscure. Members of the liberation forces recall learning of the word and how to **toyi-toyi** in the camps in Egypt where members of *uMkhonto weSizwe* (MK) and Zipra were trained together. It was used to describe the combined singing and strenuous physical training that stretched over many hours. Later it came to be used to inspire commitment and solidarity at political rallies and in public demonstrations.

Theories as to the origin of the word abound. One surmise, attractive to those who believe in the influence and richness of English, is that it is an African adaptation of the English word 'toy', when 'toying' is used to mean dealing with someone carelessly, if not mockingly. Subsequently it has been absorbed into southern African English in this evolved form.

> The **toyi-toyi** is a kind of ritual war dance performed with particular zest when there are television crews present.
> The **toyi-toyiers** move fluidly forward with harmonious purpose.
> The act of **toyi-toying** is inspirational to the participants and serves to unite the group in its purpose and resolve.

See: **Foreign words**

Tragedy

Tragedy refers to a dramatic representation of significant and serious events which have catastrophic effects on the protagonist. Aristotle defined tragedy as 'the imitation of an action that is serious and also, having magnitude, complete in itself'. Tragedy presents 'incidents arousing pity and fear'.

Transformations

According to a theory of grammar called transformational generative grammar, English sentences have two phrase structures: a deep structure and one which comes from it called the surface structure. Understanding of deep structures helps to clarify why a complex sentence is wrong when, for example, it has no verb.

A deep structure becomes a surface structure by a process called a transformation. Many transformations are possible, but common ones include question, negative, contraction, passive and relative clause transformations.

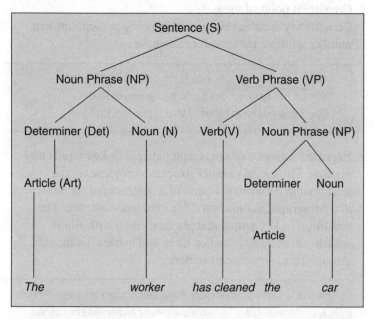

Deep Structure:
 The worker has cleaned the car.
Negative transformation:
 The worker has **not** cleaned the car.
Contraction transformation:
 The worker **hasn't** cleaned the car.
Passive transformation:
 The car hasn't **been cleaned by** the worker.
Question transformation:
 Hasn't the car been cleaned by the worker?

Transition

Transitions are bridges which carry the reader from one sentence or paragraph to another. Thus, coherence is achieved. The relationships between sentences and paragraphs are strengthened by four devices.

1. Consistent point of view
Consistency is achieved by not changing person, tense or number within a paragraph or sentence.

> X **One** does not have to look far to find **your** mistake.
> √ You do not have to look far to find your mistake.
> √ One does not have to look far to find one's mistake.

2. Repeated sentence or paragraph patterns or key words and phrases. The use of parallel structures emphasizes the relationship between the parts of a sentence, or the sentences in a paragraph, to the central idea or topic sentence. The repetition of key words and phrases, often with slight modification, stresses major ideas and carries the thought through from sentence to sentence.

> There is a sadness associated with every road accident. There is a crime of neglect or carelessness or recklessness behind each crash. There is a failure evident in human nature which glares at us from every car smash.

3. Pronoun reference
Pronouns tie sentences or paragraphs together. By substituting for nouns, pronouns repeat the noun concept without duplicating the word. Each pronoun makes the reader think back to the original noun. For this device to be successful, there must never be any doubt about which noun the pronoun replaces.

> Portia: The quality of mercy is not strain'd,
>   **It** droppeth as the gentle rain from heaven
>   Upon the place beneath: **it** is twice bless'd;
>   **It** blesseth **him** that gives and **him** that takes:
>   **'T**is mightiest in the mightiest: **it** becomes
>   The throned monarch better than **his** crown ...
>
> The Merchant of Venice (IV(i), 180-185)

4. Use of transitional words and phrases
Transitional expressions show how various points, ideas or events are related to one another. These coordinating expressions are vital in the process of communicating, but they must be used sparingly.

The following list of common transitional words and phrases has been arranged around the relationships they point to.

- **Transitional words to indicate addition**
  additionally, again, also and, and then, besides, beyond that, equally important, finally, first, further, furthermore, in addition, last, likewise, moreover, next, second, third, too, over and above.

- **Transitional words to indicate cause and effect**
  accordingly, as a result, consequently, for that reason, hence, inevitable, in short, necessarily, otherwise, then, therefore, thus, truly.

- **Transitional words to indicate comparison**
  in a like manner, in the same way, likewise, similarly.

- **Transitional words to indicate concession**
  after all, although this may be true, at the same time, even though, I admit, naturally, of course.

- **Transitional words to indicate contrast**
  after all, although true, and yet, at the same time, be that as it may, but, for all that, however, in contrast, in spite of, nevertheless,

notwithstanding, on the contrary, on the other hand, still, yet.

- **Transitional words to indicate place**
  above that, at this point, below that, beyond that, here, there, near, next to that, on the other side, outside, within.

- **Transitional words to indicate special features or examples or emphasis**
  above all, certainly, especially, for example, for instance, incidentally, indeed, in fact, in other words, in particular, specifically, that is, to illustrate, surely.

- **Transitional words to indicate summary**
  as has been noted, in brief, in conclusion, in other words, in short, on the whole, to conclude, to summarize, to sum up.

- **Transitional words to indicate time relations**
  after a short time, afterwards, as long as, as soon as, at last, at length, at that time, at the same time, before, earlier, immediately, in the meantime, lately, later, meanwhile, of late, presently, shortly, since, soon, suddenly, temporarily, thereafter, thereupon, until, when, while.

Vary the use of transitional expressions, as their repetition detracts from the point rather than enhancing an argument. However, the judicious use of transitional words and phrases will help your reader follow your line of thought from one idea to the next.

Transitive

A **transitive verb** is one that takes an object.

Laurel loves Jan.	Mosa presented the course.
Vicki has a new kitten.	Coco hates school.

An **intransitive verb** does not take an object.

> Summer has arrived.
> Joss died.

Some verbs may look intransitive, in that they have no obvious object in the sentence. However, you can test whether the verb is transitive by asking 'what?' or 'whom?' after the verb.

> Leon shaves every morning.
> *Leon shaves what? (His chin, his face, his legs?)*

If the verb is truly intransitive, the question 'what?' or 'whom?' would not make sense.

> Leon struggles every morning
> *(Leon struggles what? would not make sense; therefore 'struggles' is an intransitive verb.)*

Trite ideas

Trite ideas are wornout, superficial expressions of concepts that are stale and everyday. Triteness is an indication that the writer has not thought at all deeply about her topic, but is merely annotating second-hand ideas in tired language. A trite piece of writing is about as exciting as a plate of dusty cardboard-tasting biscuits, emptied out of a six-month old biscuit packet. Any writer who wants to make an impact on her audience will strive for original ideas and fresh, effective expression.

The following pieces of students' writing are examples of triteness.

> X   I really think that each person is unique. We all have our own special talents and we all have good and bad in us. Some people are, of course, nicer than others, but we should never judge our fellow man without putting ourselves in his shoes first.
>
> X   Our end-of-year office party was a real success. Everyone really enjoyed the delicious food, and socializing with one's colleagues makes a pleasant change from the usual dog-eat-dog atmosphere. As everyone needs a chance to unwind, and a good time was had by all, I think it is a good idea to have parties on a more regular basis.

The major drawback of trite writing is that it usually consists of empty, meaningless generalizations and thus does not tell your reader anything. As the point of writing is communication, writers should rather be specific, detailed, and accurate than vague, general and nebulous in their expressions.

See: **Clichés**

Try to, try and

Try to is the correct form, as the verb (try) needs to be followed by a preposition (to). 'And' is not a preposition, but a conjunction, which joins two statements or pieces of information.

> Please try to do this properly for a change.

U

Un-, in-

Un- and **in-** are negative prefixes. They become part of the words to which they are attached and are therefore not used with a hyphen unless the words to which they are linked begin with capital letters.

> un- + like = unlike
> in- + disputable = indisputable
> un- + do = undo
> in- + direct = indirect
> un- + American = un-American

In- is the strongest negative prefix.

> un- + happy = unhappy (or one who is not happy)
> in- + describable = indescribable (or something beyond description)

See: **In-, un-; Prefixes**

Underlining

Underlining is used in cases where the writer is unable to use italics (for example, in handwritten essays, or when using a typewriter or printer which does not print italics).

See: **Italics; Referencing**

305

Understatement

Understatement (also called **litotes**) and overstatement (also called **hyperbole**) are figurative devices in which there is a disjunction between the importance a writer seems to put on a statement, and its actual importance.

Understatement occurs when a writer downplays or understresses an important statement.

Overstatement occurs when a writer overstresses or exaggerates the importance of a statement.

See: **Hyperbole**

Uninterested

Uninterested means 'without interest', while **disinterested** means 'impartial'.

> Good judges are disinterested but not uninterested.

See: **Disinterested**

Unity

A unified paragraph is one that has a single, clear purpose. All of the sentences in the paragraph clearly relate to that purpose, which is usually stated in a single sentence called the topic sentence.

See: **Paragraphs; Topic sentences**

Us, we

Us is used as part of the object of a sentence, while **we** refers to those carrying out the action described.

306

> **We** play tennis every weekend. *(subject)*
> The dog followed **us** home. *(object)*

Some people have difficulty with multiple subjects or objects, although the rule remains the same.

> As it was so cold, the animals and **we** snuggled together. *(subject)*
> The teachers spoke to the pupils and **us**. *(object)*

See: **Case; Person; Pronouns**

Usage

This refers to the generally accepted way in which a language is used. Obviously, care must be taken not to confuse **use** and **usage**.

> After deciding on the correct usage, he knew which word to use.

Use to, used to

Use to is sometimes mistaken for **used to**.

> I use the car to go to work.
> I used to be very fond of driving.

V

Variety

Variety is the spice of life. This proverb applies directly to writing. A limited range of vocabulary may lead to the repetition of words and phrases. The message or idea may be clear, but the writing may seem dull because it lacks variety, which is often achieved by the use of alternative words or phrases.

> X A great groan was made by the great crowd.
>
> *This sentence can be improved simply by eliminating the repetition.*
>
> A great groan was made by the large crowd.

See: **Repetition; Synonyms**

Verbs

A verb is a 'doing' word. It expresses an action or a state of being.

> Thandi **likes** cooking.
> Sibongile **sings** like an angel.
> Andries **reads** many books.
> Joe **is** in the army.

A verb is the key element of sentences and clauses, and no string of words is a full, complete sentence unless it contains a finite verb.

Verbs have five forms – the base, the infinitive, the present participle, the past participle, and the past tense form.

Base		hope	drink
Infinitive	to + base	to hope	to drink
Present Participle	base + ing	hoping	drinking
Past Participle	base + ed	hoped	drank
	(or + en)		
Past Tense Form	base + ed	hoped	drunk

A verb is **regular** if its past tense and past participle are the same, and are regularly formed using the rules. ('Hope' is a regular verb.) If the two forms differ, and do not follow the rules, the verb is **irregular**. ('Drink' is an irregular verb.) The forms of irregular verbs have to be learnt off by heart if the verbs are to be used correctly. Irregular forms are usually given in a dictionary.

Base	go	do	be	see	shake
Infinitive	to go	to do	to be	to see	to shake
Present Participle	going	doing	being	seeing	shaking
Past Participle	gone	done	been	seen	shaken
Past Tense Form	went	did	was / were	saw	shook

See: **Active, passive; Anomalous finite verbs; Auxiliary verbs; -ed, -t; Participles; Sentences; -t, -ed; Tenses;Transitive**

Verbosity

See: **Wordiness**

Verse

Verse describes compositions written in regular rhythmical

patterns, or metre. (Prose, on the other hand, is language written as we ordinarily speak it, with no recurrent units of rhythm.) Both poetry and drama can be written in verse form.

Verse can be rhymed or unrhymed. **Blank verse** is verse made up of unrhymed lines written in the rhythmical pattern (or metre) called iambic pentameter.

Free verse is verse which has only occasional units of recurring rhythmical patterns.

See: **Metre; Rhyme**

Very

Very is an intensifier.

> Grandpa is very interested in stamps.
> I am very dissatisfied with your work.

Very cannot be used with comparative adjectives or adverbs. **Much** should be used instead. **Very** can, however, be used with superlative adjectives.

See: **Adjectives (Degrees of Comparison); Comparisons**

> She is much happier.
> He is much better.
> I like the new house much more than I did the old one.
>
> This is my very best wine.

Very much can only be used to intensify past participles functioning as verbs.

> He was very much offended by your remark.

See: **Intensifiers**

Viz

An abbreviation of the Latin word *videlicet* (one may see), **viz** means 'namely' or 'in other words'. It is usually used to introduce an explanation or elaboration of a point made previously. Modern writing usually replaces **viz** with **namely**. When it appears in writing, it is read aloud as 'namely'.

> In Durban, hotels have few vacancies during the school summer holidays, viz in December and early January.

See: **Abbreviations**

Vogue words

These are words or expressions that happen to be 'in fashion', and are used so often and in so many different contexts that they lose something of their original strength and meaning. When writing, choose words that are suited to both your reader and your subject.

See: **Audience; Clichés; Register**

Vowels

In the English alphabet there are, traditionally, five vowels (**a e i o u**). (The other letters are consonants.) Apart from the letters of the alphabet, though, there are as many as twelve vowel 'sounds'.

See: **Consonants**

Vowels play a significant role in English: a vowel is the crucial constituent of a syllable, for example, and assonance – a poetic device – is based on the repetition of vowel sounds.

See: **Assonance; Hyphenation; Syllable**

When / where

When and **where** are relative pronouns. **When** introduces an adverb clause of time and is also used to ask questions about time.

> I'll pay the bill when I have the money.
> I was on the telephone when the doorbell rang.
>
> When will you be home?
> When do you write your exam?

Where introduces adverb clauses of place and is also used to ask questions about place.

> I left the key where I found it.
>
> Where did you put the keys?
> Where are you spending your holidays?

Whether, if

Whether is generally used to indicate alternatives.

> I am not sure whether to invest my bonus in a holiday or in my overdraft.

See: **Whether ... or**

If is used to indicate uncertainty.

> I don't know if it will rain.
> I don't know if I can face another four-hour staff meeting.

Whether ... or

Whether .... or are correlative conjunctions.

> Whether we go out, or stay at home, we still have to put up with
> each other's company.
> Whether you like it or not, you have to abide by the speed limit.

See: **Conjunctions; Correlative conjunctions; Whether, if**

Which

Which is a relative pronoun, used to ask questions about people and things. **Which** is normally used when there is a limited choice, while **what** is used for a larger, almost unlimited choice.

> Which of your two parents influenced you the most?
> Which type of pencil do you prefer – B, HB, or H?
>
> What colour is your car?
> What is your lucky number?

As a relative pronoun within a sentence, **which** joins clauses together by referring back to a noun or pronoun in the initial clause. ('Which' refers to things, while 'who' and 'whom' refer to people.)

> Unisa, which teaches by correspondence, is the biggest
> university in South Africa.

313

While

While is used in the sense of 'during the time that ...'.

> While the vegetables were cooking, we played a hand of cards.

While can also mean much the same as 'although'.

> While I agree with you, I do not think it is worth complaining.

When a sense of comparison is needed, the correct word to use is **whilst**.

> He plays rugby in a short-sleeved jersey, whilst I prefer a long-sleeved one.

Who, whom, whose, who's

Who, **whom**, and **whose** are all relative pronouns. They can be used to join clauses together by referring back to nouns in the first clause.

Who, **whom**, and **whose** are used to refer to people, while 'which' is used for things. **Whom** refers to the object of a verb or preposition.

See: **Which**

> This is the woman who will replace me as secretary.
> This is the secretary whose job you will be taking over while she is on maternity leave.
> Where is the man to whom I spoke yesterday?
> One should remain faithful to the person to whom one is married.

Whose is the possessive case, while **who's** is the contracted form of 'who is'.

> I had to phone the student whose assignment I had lost.
> David, whose wife is ill in bed, is doing all the cooking.
>
> Mike, who's at a health farm at present, will be back at work next week.

All these relative pronouns can also be used to ask questions.

> Who is going to pay the bill?
> To whom shall I send the bill?
> Whose responsibility is it to pay the bill?
> Who's going to pay the bill?

Will

See: **Shall**

Wordiness

Wordiness is the excessive use of a great number of words to say something which can be more effectively and simply stated in fewer words.

> They invited me to go and close up again – Now the fact is I don't want to – I actually feel quite emotional here, you know – I mean we meet these guys, a lot of them have done very horrendous things – some of them give us flam excuses for things they've done, things you wouldn't believe in a month of Sundays – But many of them say openly: 'I murdered a person for this reason or that reason, and this is why I'm here,' and you make friends with them – That also sounds corny – We've had a-one-rushed-day, but you see people, you talk to people, you look at their eyes ... and, uh, I don't want to go and lock them up again – And I stick to the view that, um, hey, man!,

315

> people do awful things and I'm not saying that it's a very rosy
> world but there's a way beyond this to punish people, a way
> beyond this incarceration, and those guys who wanna say it's a
> holiday camp and they wanna pooh-pooh and they wanna laugh
> and they wanna say prison's no penalty – Hey, look, even this
> little experience of a day sitting around here, you realize it's a
> penalty, you don't need to beat the guy and kick him and make
> him live in degraded, subhuman circumstances – It's penalty,
> this is Penalty with a capital P, man, and you feel it when you're
> here. Thanks.
>
> Denis Beckett on *Beckett's Trek* (SATV), after visiting a prison.

Wordiness can lead to misunderstanding and confusion. The
above quote had to be followed by the simpler, shorter, clearer
explanation below:

> Denis says that if you think he's an idealist halfwit wanting
> criminals let out to rape and rob, forget it. Prisons don't
> stop crime. Let's try new ways.
>
> Notice on *Beckett's Trek*, to clarify his earlier statement.

Redundancy (using two or more words which repeat the same
information) is one type of wordiness. 'A *true* fact', 'a
personal friend', '*living* incarnation', '*completely* finished',
'regress *back* to' are all examples of wordy and redundant
phrases. The italicized words add no extra meaning and could
easily be eliminated.

Euphemisms also lead to wordiness. Unpleasant ideas need
not always be cushioned in excess verbiage. To refer to
prostitutes, for example, as 'members of the oldest
profession', or to death as 'meeting one's maker' or 'going to
one's eternal reward', or to divorce as 'a parting of the ways'
makes your writing sound evasive and insincere.

Gobbledygook, or using many words in the place of one, and using multi-syllable words where a single syllable would do, is much favoured by politicians and bureaucrats, as in the following examples:

X Due to the fact that hydro-electric generation of electrical current now involves costly materials and operations, it is respectfully requested that personnel be assiduous in ascertaining that all electrical appliances, particularly those used for illumination, are turned off if not in use.

Meaning: Since electricity is expensive, please turn off the lights.

In 1986, George Schultz, then American Secretary of State, gave the following wordy answer to the question 'Do you consider the African National Congress a terrorist organization? And if not, why not?'

X Schultz replied: 'There are also others with different instincts, and I thought that one of the most interesting things of the report I got, anyway, from the leaders of the Eminent Persons Group, who I hope can say engaged – maybe they will decide they can't be, but if they can, I think they have been very constructive – but they talked to Mr Mandela at length, they talked to various black leaders in and out of South Africa and in the ANC, and their judgement is – whether their judgement would be borne out in the event or not, no one can say for sure – but their judgement was – as reported to me – that what these people that they talked to were willing to do was engage in a dialogue and a negotiation if there was a reasonable chance of something genuinely substantive coming out of it, and to do their best to work against violence in that setting.'

Pretoria News

Word order

The basic word order in English sentences is subject-verb.

To this may be added a direct object, in the order subject-verb-object.

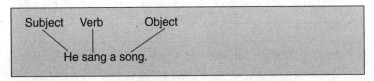

An indirect object can come between the verb and the object in the order subject-verb-indirect object-direct object.

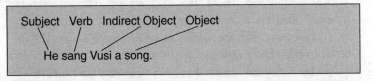

If the indirect object comes after the verb, a preposition must be used.

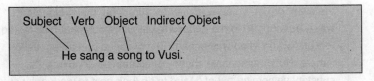

Placing modifiers in the correct place in sentences often causes problems.

Adverbs can be placed –
• before the verb

> He **suddenly** sang Vusi a song.

- at the end of the clause

> He sang Vusi a song **suddenly**.

- at the beginning of the clause

> **Suddenly**, he sang Vusi a song.

Adjectives must be placed next to the noun they modify. See the entry on adjectives for the ordering of multiple adjectives.

> He sang Vusi a **sentimental** song.

See: **Awkward phrasing; Indirect speech; Questions; Sentences; Split infinitive; Subject, Object**

Words

The English language contains close to a million words. Such richness is both a blessing and a curse. Some words are interchangeable; others, while seemingly similar, have important distinctions in meaning.

> I saw someone.
> I saw an individual.
> *The sentences above are similar in meaning.*
>
> They live in poverty.
> They live in want.
> *While the second sentence implies that they live in need of things, the first means that they are poor.*

Normally the shortest word is the best, provided that it has the intended meaning. ('End', for example, is better than 'terminate'.) The context in which a word is used, however, may sometimes require the longer word.

See: **Feeling in words; Shades of meaning; Synonyms**

Would of

Would of and 'could of' are incorrect phonetic transcriptions of **would've** and 'could've'. Avoid this error by writing the words out in full: **would have** and 'could have'.

See: **Contractions**

Would, should

Would is used for something that will, may, or might happen if certain conditions are met ('She would help you if you asked her') and for emphasis ('He would take the car just when I need it!').

Should is the past tense of shall. It is also used to indicate that something ought, or ought not to occur.

> I thought I should never see her again.
>
> You should attempt to do this on your own.
> You should not always rely on other people.

In British and South African usage **should** is used with 'I' and 'we', to express a wish or desire.

> I should love to have a new motor car.

320

Wrong words

Use each word in its proper sense. Choosing the right word –
or not choosing the wrong one – is a difficulty for writers,
especially for those who are less experienced.

The following guidelines are useful.
- Be idiomatic.
- Use colloquial words only when speaking.
- Use standard English words.

However, these guidelines are helpful only if you know what
is meant by idiomatic, colloquial or standard English. Such
knowledge comes slowly, after much reading and experience.
Until you achieve a high level of competence in English,
consult a good dictionary whenever you write.

The list of words which follows contains examples of words
that are often misused. Those marked with an asterisk (*) are
explained in this handbook. Refer to a good dictionary to
clarify your understanding of the words about which you are
uncertain.

a, an *	ingenious, ingenuous
accept, except*	lay, lie*
affect, effect*	learn, teach*
agree to, agree with	lend, borrow*
allusion, illusion*	less, few*
already, all ready*	lightening, lightning
amount, number*	negligent, negligible
complement, compliment*	official, officious
continual, continuous*	practice, practise*
credible, credulous	principal, principle*
disinterested, uninterested*	raise, rise*
eligible, illegible	recourse, resource
explicit, implicit	sociable, social
hanged, hung*	stationary, stationery
industrial, industrious	that, which*
infer, imply*	there, their*

Yahoo

The word is derived from *Gulliver's Travels* by Jonathan Swift, and is used when referring to someone who is crude, coarse or obscene. It is generally used colloquially.

You and I

Uncertainty about the verb-ending is sometimes the result of combining **you and I** as the multiple subject of a sentence. There is no problem in the following sentence:

> You and I are playing together.

The uncertainty lies in the use of 'either ... or' and 'neither ... nor' in combination with **you and I**. These conjunctions cause 'you' and 'I' to be regarded separately. The correct verb-form is thus singular in such a sentence.

> Either you or I **am** playing.

The reality, however, is that usage is moving towards the grammatically incorrect form: 'Either you or I are driving.'

See: **Either ... or; Neither ... nor**

Many English speakers feel that **I** is the correct use in all cases, and that there is something 'wrong' with **me**. **You and me** is, in fact, the correct form in the object position of a sentence, or after a preposition.

> He said he would pay you and me tomorrow.
> She asked if she could give the report to you and me to handle.

Yours

Yours is not used with an apostrophe. It is a possessive pronoun and, like 'his', 'hers' and 'its', takes no apostrophe.

> This book is yours, that book is hers.

See: **Apostrophe; Pronouns**

Z

Z or S

There is no general agreement about the endings **-ise** and **-ize**, as even the major publishers differ. Originally all words of Greek derivation used **-ize**, and American usage also favours the **-ize** ending. Writers may choose either, but need to be consistent.

See: **-ize, -ise; Spelling**

Index

A 41
Abbreviations 7, 8, 42,
    105, 113, 122, 146,
    175, 184, 265, 271,
    311
Absolute adjectives 19
Abstract nouns 9, 13,
    281
Abstract words 172
Abstractions 11, 42
Academic essays 9
Academic reading 75
Academic writing 244,
    249
Accent 225
Accents 11
Accept 12, 123
Accommodation 13
Account for 155
Acknowledgement 207,
    241, 245
Acronyms 8, 13, 74
Action, continuous 289
Action, habitual 288
Actions 10
Active verbs 211
Active voice 14, 210
AD 8
Address, formal 227
Address, terms of 60
Addresses 15
Adjectival clauses 65
Adjectival constructions
    106
Adjectival suffixes 17
Adjectives 10, 16, 18,
    19, 26, 28, 29, 34, 41,
    74, 94, 96, 125, 126,
    150, 152, 157, 173,

179, 209, 216, 256,
    261, 280, 281
    absolute 19
    age 17
    colour 17
    comparative 105, 292
    condition 17
    degrees of
        comparison 72
    derivation 17
    evaluative 17
    material 17
    measurement 17
    multiple 319
    origin 17
    participial 167
    shape 17
    size 17
    subjective 17
    superfluous 54
    superlative 310
    uncomparable 019
Adverb of manner 275
Adverb phrases 106
Adverbial clauses 66
Adverbs 19, 26, 70, 74,
    95, 152, 157, 238,
    275, 280, 282
    comparative 292
    superfluous 54
Advertisements 7, 27
Advice 19
Advise 19
Adviser 19
Advisory 19
Affect 19
Affectation 21, 264
Affective factors 21
Affirmative

antecedents 23
Affixes 9, 22, 97
Afrikanerisms 154, 167
Age adjectives 17
Agreement 39, 44, 108,
    113, 118, 119, 191
    pronouns 22, 23
    subject 23
    verb 23
Alibi 25
All 26
All ready 26
All together 26
All ways 26
Alliteration 27, 130
Allude 27
Allusion 28
Almost 28
Already 26
Alternate 29
Alternative 29
Altogether 26
Always 26
Am 32
Ambiguity 30, 48, 94
American English 31,
    93, 136, 141, 159,
    160, 218, 222, 267
Among 31
Amongst 31
Amount 32
Ampersand 9, 32
Amphibrach 178
An 33, 41
Analogy 33
Analyze 155
Analysis 202
Analysis, literary 162,
    178

Anapaest 178
And 34
Anglicized words 35
Anno Domini 8
Anomalous finite verbs 35, 153
Antecedents 22, 23, 38
Anticlimax 50
Antonyms 38
Any one 38
Anybody 38
Anyone 38
Apostrophe 7, 40, 86, 114, 117, 139, 200, 323
Arabic numerals 192
Archaic words 294
Argument 296
Argument, essays 120
Arise 243
Articles 10, 13, 98, 129
  definite 41, 95, 293
  indefinite 7, 33, 41, 151
Articles, titles of 61
As 43, 170
Assonance 43, 130, 311
Asterisks 133
Attitude 129
Attributes 18
Attributes, concrete 11
Audience 44, 114, 249
Auditory imagery 27
Authentic speech 100
Autobiography 45
Auxiliaries, modal 46
Auxiliary verbs 36, 45, 46, 135, 153, 175, 208, 235, 261,286
Awkward constructions 24
Awkward phrasing 48
Awkward writing 42

Balanced structures 108
Barbarisms 217
Bathos 50

BBC English 276
BC 8
Before Christ 8
Beside 50
Between 31, 51
Bias 138, 242, 258
  sexist 39, 123
Bibliography 51, 245
Biennial 51
Biography 52
Book titles 61, 159, 295
Borrow 52, 168
Borrowed nouns 272
Brackets 53, 241
Brand names 62
Brevity 54
British English 141, 160, 266, 320
British usage 31
Business letters 9, 55, 168, 244, 255
Business writing 55
But 58, 143

Can 59
Cannon 60
Canon 59
Capital letters 9, 13, 42, 60, 105, 164, 184, 257, 305
Case 62
  objective 64
  possessive 64, 139, 217, 314
  pronouns 115
Catalectic lines 180
Catharsis 64
Cause and effect 301
Certainty 47
Changes in language 165, 266
Chronological relationships 203
Cinema 64
Classic comedy 69
Classicism 65
Classification 202, 209

Classification, Dewey decimal 99
Clauses 38, 42, 43, 65, 70, 84, 171, 258
  dependent 136
  detached 136
  detached dependent 136
  independent 115, 137
  main 280
  relative 70
  subordinate 119, 280
Cliché 66, 148, 168, 244
Close reading 74
Clumsy expression 67, 255
Codes, postal 15
Coherence 250
Collective nouns 25, 67
Colloquial speech 19, 38, 64, 276
Colloquial writing 39
Colloquialisms 44, 48, 68, 99, 118, 123, 126, 141, 249, 263, 292
Colons 69, 93, 240
Colour adjectives 017
Combination words 292
Combinations, subject-verb 149
Comedy 69
Comma 117
Comma splice 71, 115, 117
Commands 149, 257
Commas 9, 58, 70, 101, 146, 239
  inverted 101, 238
Common errors 113, 140, 150, 163, 238
Common usage 41
Communication, complete 122
Communication, unambiguous 277

Communications, specialist 161
Comparative adjectives 105, 292
Comparative adverbs 292
Comparative forms 109
Compare 155
Comparison 262, 301, 314
  contrast 202
  degrees of 18. 72
  description by 97
  double 105
Comparisons 31
  figurative 72
Complaint, letters of 56
Complement 48, 63, 153
  subjective 63
Complete
  communication 122
  expression 257
  ideas 134
Completed events 290
Complex ideas 118
Compound nouns 140, nouns 215
Compound prepositions 106
Compound sentences 71, 258
Compound tenses 153
Compound words 73, 144
Compounds 026
Comprehension 74
Computer terms 74
Concave 83
Concepts 10, 11, 33, 67
Concession 301
Conciseness 54, 119
Concrete attributes 11
Concrete writing 121
Condensed form 218
Condition 183
Condition adjectives 17

Conditional possibility 47
Conditional structure 148
Confirmation, request for 236
Conjunctions 43, 171
  coordinating 34, 58, 84, 115
  correlative 52, 84, 88, 108, 187, 189, 243, 313
  subordinating 84, 135, 280
Connectives
  coordinating 135
  subordinating 135
Connectors, logical 84
Connotation 127, 284
Connotations, symbolic 283
Consider 155
Consonant groups 283
Consonant sounds 41, 44
Consonantal sounds 27
Consonants 7, 33, 84, 208, 213, 269, 282, 311
Construction 31
Constructions 200
  active 15
  adjectival 106
  awkward 24
  direct 150
  impersonal 149
  passive 15, 211
Context 23, 58, 85, 124, 173
Context, formal 25
Continual 85
Continuity 85
Continuous 85
Continuous action 289
Contractions 7, 37, 40, 86, 113, 160
Contrast 156, 158, 301

Contrast-comparison 202
Contrasting ideas 143
Conversational English 171
Convex 83
Convoluted expressions 168
Coordinating conjunctions 34, 58, 84, 115
Coordinating connectives 135
Correct arrangement, words 284
Correlative conjunctions 52, 84, 88, 108, 187, 189, 243, 313
Countable nouns 32, 174
Creative writing 129
Critical 156
Criticize 156
Criticism, practical 88, 111
Curriculum vitae 89

Dactyl 178
Dangling modifiers 92, 115, 118, 280
Dash 92, 133, 145, 240
Dates 93, 193
Dead metaphors 66, 178
Decimals 193
Deep structure 298
Definite articles 41, 95, 293
Definitions 69
Degree of comparison
  comparative 18
  positive 18
  superlative 18
Degrees of comparison 72
Deity, reference to 62
Delusion 28

327

Index

Demonstrative
  pronouns 95, 98, 223
Denotation 127
Denotative meaning
  283
Dependant 096
Dependent clauses 65,
  136
Derivation, adjectives
  17
Derivation, words 9
Derivational affix 97
Describe 156
Description 296
  by comparison 97
  by example 97
  by function 97
  by synthesis 97
Detached clauses 136
Detached phrases 136
Determination 261
Determiners 17, 97, 147
Devices
  dramatic 265
  figurative 306
  metrical 027
  poetical 111, 201,
  311
Dewey classification 99
Dialect 99
Dialects 276
Dialogue 86, 100, 102,
  103
Dictionary entries 101
Dictionary meaning 283
Dimeter 179
Diminutives 281
Direct constructions
  150
Direct object 166, 197
Direct questions 235
Direct speech 60, 100,
  102, 118
Discuss 156
Disinterested 104, 306
Dissertation 294
Distorted meaning 110

Double comparison 105
Double quotation marks
  240
Double-barrelled names
  164
Draft, essays 120
Drama 69, 103, 105,
  226
Dramatic devices 265
Dramatic overstatement
  144
Dramatic representation
  298
Due to 105

E-mail 7
Each 39, 107
Earlier past 291
Editing 251
Effect 19
Effective 21
Elaboration 168
Elder 109, 199
Electronic sources 247
Elements 48
Ellipsis 109, 241
Elude 27
Embarrass 110
Emigrate 110
Emotion 264
Emotional significance
  283
Emotions 010
Emotive language 128
Emphasis 28, 38, 45,
  123, 159, 177, 302
End rhyme 252
End-stopped lines 112
Endorse 111
Enjambment 111
Enquiry, letters of 55
Envelopes 15
Epic 112
Erotica 113
Errors, common 113,
  140, 150, 163, 238
  unconscious 226

Essays
  abbreviations 122
  academic 9
  acknowledgement
  207
  argument 120
  audience 44, 114,
  249
  bibliography 51
  brackets 53
  brevity 54
  canon 59
  clumsy expression 67
  common errors 113
  comparison 97
  comprehension 74
  conclusion 120
  concrete writing 121
  contrast 158
  description 97
  direct speech 100
  editing 251
  electronic sources
  247
  example 97
  first draft 120
  footnotes 131, 207
  formulation 74
  function 97
  generalizations 117,
  139
  illogical shifts 119
  instruction words 155
  introduction 120, 157
  italics 295
  literary criticism 252
  logic 117
  logical order 202
  major ideas 120
  metaphors 66
  middle paragraphs
  120
  natural order 202
  numbers 54
  order 121
  organization 117, 202
  paragraphs 101, 120,

157, 205, 295
paraphrase 206
parentheses 53
planning 119
practical criticism 88
proofreading 67, 226
proportion 226
punctuation 117, 132, 233, 239, 257
quotations 53, 121, 131, 240
reader 44
realism 244
references 131, 194, 244, 295
register 44, 248
research 99, 120, 121
revision 121, 250
rhetoric 251
sentences 257
slang 118
spelling 266
spelling rules 268
style 278
supporting argument 120
synthesis 97
telegraphese 54
theme 120, 293
thesis statement 120, 158
titles 61, titles 159, titles, 295
topic 155
topic sentences 120, 158, 295
unconscious errors 226
wordiness 119, 157, 315
works cited 245
writing 120
Essence, ideas 129
Etc 113, 122
Etymology 160
Euphemism 122, 316

Evaluate 156
Evaluative adjectives 17
Evasion 14
Events, completed 290
Every 122
Everybody 39, 122
Everyone 39, 122
Exaggeration 123, 130, 144
Example, description by 97
Examples, concrete 11
Except 12, 123
Excerpt 124
Exclamation marks 101, 124, 136, 157, 239
Explain 156
Explanation 296
Explicit 125
Exposition 296
Expository prose 202
Expressions
    clumsy 67
    complete 257
    convoluted 168
    transitional 143
    vague 265

Fables 126
Fabulous 126
Factors, affective 21
Fantastic 126
Farther 127
Faulty parallelism 206
Feeling, words 127
Feelings 129
Feelings in words 284
Feminine gender 138
Fewer 128
Figurative comparisons 72
Figurative devices 306
Figurative language 129
Figures of speech 130, 144, 177, 262
Film titles 61,159
Final draft 219

Finite verbs 35, 130
First draft 120
First person pronouns 223
Flee 131
Fly 131
Footnotes 131, 207
For 134
Forceful constructions 150
Fore 134
Foreign words 132, 159, 164, 165, 266, 272, 297
Form
    condensed 218
    object 58
Formal address 227
Formal context 25
Formal language 99
Formal register 44
Formal speech 22
Formal writing 9, 22, 35, 40, 92, 122, 134, 187, 231
Formality, level of 249
Forms, comparative 109
Forms, plural 213, 273
Forms, superlative 109
Formulation 74
Four-letter words 133
Fragmentary sentences 116, 134
Free verse 310
Fulfil 136
Full rhyme 252
Full-stops 8, 54, 93, 110, 136, 239, 257
Function 209
Function, description by 97
Function, infinitive 152
Functions, grammatical 45
Further 127
Fused participles 209
Fused sentences 72, 137

Future perfect
    progressive tense 288
Future perfect tense 287
Future progressive tense
    287
Future tense 261
Future tense, simple
    286
Future time 286

Gender 22, 138
Gender-marked
    pronouns 259
Gender-neutral
    language 260
General truths 288
Generalizations 117,
    139, 172, 304
Genitive 139
Gerunds 64, 140, 153,
    209
Gobbledygook 317
Got 140
Gotten 141
Grammatical functions
    45

Habitual action 288
Hang 142
Helping verbs 36, 45
Heptameter 179
Hexameter 179
Homely 143
Homily 143
Homonyms 143
However 143
Hung 142
Hyperbole 123, 130,
    144, 306
Hypermetric lines 180
Hyphenation 73, 145,
    163, 283
Hyphens 144
Hypothesis 183

Iamb 179
Iambic verse 180

Idea, essence of 129
Ideas
    complete 134
    complex 118
    contrasting 143
    essays 120
    logical order 250
    main 295
    predominant 293
    presentation of 240
    similar 171, 206
    trite 303
    unity of 250
Idiom 31
Idiom, errors in 116
Idiomatic meaning 146
Idioms
    opaque 146
    translation of 147
    transparent 146
If 312
Illogical meaning 126
Illogical shifts 119
Illusion 28
Imagery, auditory 27
Immigrate 110
Impartiality 104
Imperative 149
Imperative mood 182
Imperfect rhyme 252
Impersonal
    constructions 149,
    200
Impersonal pronouns
    200
Implication 154
Implicit 125, 150
Implicit comparison
    262
Imply 150
Incomplete sentences
    134
Incredible 126
Indefinite articles 7, 33,
    41, 151
Indefinite pronouns 24,
    223

Independent clauses 65,
    115, 137
Independent sentences
    71
Index cards, research
    121
Indicative mood 182
Indirect object 197
Indirect questions 235
Indirect speech 103,
    151
Infer 150
Infinitive verbs 142
Infinitive, function 152
Infinitive, split 274
Infinitives 46, 152
Informal context 173
Informal speech 25
Informal writing 29, 92
Initials 8, 15
Innuendo 154
Instruction words 155
Intensifiers 19, 157,
    275, 310
Intention 286
Interjections 157
Internal rhymes 252
Interpretation 30
Interrogative pronouns
    223
Intransitive verbs 55,
    243, 303
Introduction, essay 157
Inverted commas 101,
    238
Irony 158, 256
It's 160
Italics 132, 159, 295,
    305
Items, related 108
Its 160

Jargon 161
Juxtapose 162
Juxtaposition 108
Juxtaposition, letters
    144

Kind 163
Kind of 265

Language
  changes in 141, 165, 266
  emotive 128
  figurative 129
  gender-neutral 260
  non-literal 146
  racist 242
  sexist 138, 258
  spoken 165, 257
  uninflected 188
  written 276
Lay 166, 170
Learn 166
Learned 166
Learnt 166
Legends 126
Lend 168
Less 128
Letter writing 55, 168, 227, 255
Letters
  audience 44
  business 9, 55, 168, 244
  personal 86, 169
  reader 44
  register 44, 249
  response to 56
  salutation 227, 255
Level of formality 249
Libraries 99
Licence 170
License 170
Lie 166, 170
Like 43, 170, 261
Lines
  end-stopped 112
  run-on 112
Listener 44
Literal meaning 146, 243, 283
Literary analysis 162, 178

Literary criticism 253, 254, 256, 264, 278, 293, 298
Litotes 306
Little 264
Loaded words 128
Loan 168
Loan words 265
Logic 117, 119, 171
Logical connectors 84
Logical order 202, 250
Loose 172
Lose 172
Lot of 173

Main clauses 280
Main ideas 120, 295
Main stress 11
Main verbs 130
Major ideas 120
Malapropism 174
Manner, adverb of 275
Many 173
Margin 175
Masculine gender 138
Masculine pronouns 39
May 59, 175
Meaning 12, 26, 38, 67
Meaning
  changes in 165
  denotative 283
  dictionary 283
  distorted 110
  distortion of 048
  emotion 264
  idiomatic 146
  illogical 126
  illogical shifts 119
  instruction words 155
  literal 146, 243, 283
  metaphorical 243
  negative 129, 256
  shades of 260
  words 144
Measure, units of 8
Measurement adjectives 17

Melodramatic tone 124
Memoirs 45
Memorandum 56
Metaphor 130, 177, 262
Metaphorical meaning 243
Metaphors 33, 72, 146
Metaphors, dead 66, 178
Metaphors, mixed 177
Metre 178, 278
Metrical devices 27
Might 176
Millennium 180
Misplaced modifiers 180
Misused words 25, 48, 181, 184
Mixed metaphors 177
Modal auxiliaries 46
Modification 220
Modifiers 16, 19, 41, 48, 63, 182. 318
  dangling 92, 115, 118, 280
  misplaced 180
Money 193
Monometer 179
Mood
  imperative 182
  indicative 182
  subjunctive 183
More 183
Morphemes, separate 145
Morphology 141
Most 183
Motivate 184
Much 174
Multiple adjectives 319
Music titles 61, 159
Mythical 126

Namely 311
Names 60
  brand 62
  double-barrelled 164

personal 8
regimental 257
Narration 296
Narrative poetry 186
Narrative writing 103
Natural order 202
Near rhyme 252
Nearly 28
Negation 151
Negative
antecedents 23
meaning 129, 256
prefixes 305
questions 37
statements 37, 45, 237
Negatives 35, 186, 189
Neither 187
Neuter 187
Neuter gender 138
Neutral terms 128
Newspaper writing 27
No-one 39
Nobody 39
Non sequitur 172
Non-finite verbs 130, 135
Non-literal language 146
None 188
Nor 187
Nothing 189
Noun clauses 65
Noun phrases 97
Nouns 10, 16, 19, 26, 29, 34, 38, 43, 62, 73, 96, 97, 112, 152, 157, 166, 170, 190, 256, 271
abstract 9, 13, 281
borrowed 272
collective 25, 67
compound 140, 215
countable 32, 174, 190
identical forms 214

plural 68, 114, 139, 190
possessive form 40
proper 42, 60, 265
singular 139, 190
uncountable 32, 175, 190
Novel 191
Nuances 26
Number 22, 23, 32, 147, 191
Numbered paragraphs 194
Numbers 54, 180, 192
Numbers, unspecified 225
Numerals 211
Arabic 192
Roman 192

Object 48
Object form 58
Object, direct 166, 197
Object, indirect 197
Objective case 64
Obligation 46, 203, 261
Octameter 179
Of 198
Old English words 215
Older 109, 199
On to 199
One 200
Only 200
Onomatopoeia 201
Onto 199
Opaque idioms 146
Opinion 17
Opinion, in my 154
Opinion, personal 149
Opposites 201
Order 261
ambiguous 48
essays 121
logical 202, 250
natural 202
word 31, 147, 151, 318

Ordinary verbs 36
Organization 117, 202
Origin, words 160
Ought 203
Overstatement 306
dramatic 144
Overworked words 204, 292
Owing to 105
Ownership 225

Padding 205
Paintings, titles 239
Paradox 205
Paragraphs 101, 157, 205, 300
argument 296
description 296
explanation 296
exposition 295
narration 296
numbered 194
unified 306
Parallel structure 206, 243, 300
Parallelism 118
faulty 206
Paraphrase 206
Parentheses 53
Partial rhyme 252
Participial adjectives 167
Participial phrases 207
Participle
past 46, 142
present 46
Participles 74, 140, 280
fused 209
past 18, 166, 207, 285
present 18, 207
unrelated 209
wrongly related 208
Parts of speech 11
Parts of speech 11
Parts of speech 209
Passed 210

Passive constructions 211
Passive voice 14, 208, 210
Past 210
Past participle 18, 46, 142, 166, 207, 285
Past perfect progressive tense 291
Past perfect tense 291
Past progressive tense 290
Past tense 45, 108, 140, 142, 152, 166, 285
    simple 290
Past, second 291
Pentameter 179
Perfect progressive tense, future 288
Perfect progressive tense, past 291
Perfect tense 46, 176, 208
    future 287
    past 291
    present 289
Person 22, 211
Personal letters 169
Personal names 8
Personal opinion 149
Personal pronouns 223, 257
Phrases 26, 42, 84, 171, 258
Phrases, adverb 106
Phrases
    detached 136
    noun 97
    participial 207
    possessive 68
    prepositional 43, 73, 199
    transitional 135
Phrasing, awkward 48
Place 302
Placenames 61, 163
Plagiarism 212

Planning, essays 119
Plays 103
Plural forms 213, 273
Plural nouns 68, 114, 139
Plural pronouns 23, 123
Plural subject 23
Plural verbs 24, 188, 263
Plurals 8, 39, 40, 53, 73, 93, 133
Poem titles 61, 239
Poetical devices 111, 201, 311
Poetry 252
    catalectic lines 180
    epic 112
    hypermetric lines 180
    metre 178
    narrative 186
    scanning 179
    simile 263
    stanza 278
Point in time 217
Pornography 113
Portrait 217
Portray 217
Positive degree of comparison 18
Positive statements 237
Possessive apostrophe 114
Possessive case 64, 139, 217, 314
Possessive noun form 40
Possessive phrases 68
Possessive pronouns 40, 98, 160, 223, 323
Possibility 176
    conditional 47
    theoretical 47
Postal codes 15
Practical criticism 88, 111, 252, 254, 264, 278, 293, 298
Practical criticism,

excerpt 124
Practice 218
Practise 218
Précis 218, 282
Predicate 135, 220, 257
Prediction 286
Predominant ideas 293
Prefixes 97, 201, 220, 305
Prejudiced thinking 242
Prepositional phrases 43, 73, 199
Prepositions 12, 51, 63, 123, 134, 170, 221, 261
Prepositions, compound 106
Present participles 18, 46, 207
Present perfect tense 289
Present progressive tense 289
Present tense 45, 152
Present tense, progressive 289
Present tense, simple 288
Present time 288
Presentation of ideas 240
Primary stress 11
Principal 222
Principle 222
Principle of unity 296
Probability 47
Program 222
Programme 222
Progressive tense
    future 287
    future perfect 288
    past 290
    perfect past 291
    present 289
Prohibitions 149
Pronoun reference 30, 300

Pronoun, possessive
    323
Pronouns 16, 26, 43, 60,
    62, 122, 134, 151,
    170
    agreement 22, 23
    case 115
    demonstrative 95, 98,
        223
    first person 223
    gender-marked 259
    impersonal 200
    indefinite 24
    indefinite 223
    interrogative 223
    masculine 39
    personal 223, 257
    plural 23, 123
    possessive 40, 98,
        160, 223
    reflexive 223
    relative 38, 135, 138,
        223, 280, 312, 315
    second person 223
    self 257
    singular 22, 23, 38,
        39, 122, 138
    third person 223
    third person singular
        138
    unrelated 115
Pronunciation 12, 85,
    87, 107, 225, 266,
    276, 297
Proofreading 67, 226
Proper nouns 42, 60,
    265
Proportion 226
Propositions 171, 294
Prose writing 114, 202
Prose, expository 202
Protagonist 226, 298
Protocol 184, 226
Proverbs 231
Public speaking 231
Punctuation 15, 69, 70,
    72, 101, 117, 124,

    132, 136, 137, 144,
    157, 233, 239, 257

Qualification 220
Qualities 10, 18
Quantity 264
Question marks 136,
    235
Question words 236
Questions 36, 45, 50,
    74, 88, 197, 224, 235,
    257, 315
    essay 156
    negative 37
    reported 237
    tag 37, 236
Quicker 238
Quite 238
Quotation marks 235,
    238, 295
Quotations 53, 69, 109,
    121, 131, 206, 240

Racial bias 242
Racist language 242
Raise 243
Rank, titles of 61
Rather 243
Re 244
Reader 44
Reader 114
Reading 74
Realism 244
Reality 11
Received pronunciation
    276
Redundancy 316
Reference books 7
Reference, pronouns 30,
    300
References 99, 131, 194
Referencing 244, 295
Reflexive pronouns 223
Regimental names 257
Register 44, 248
Regular rhythm 253
Regular verbs 35

Related items 108
Relationship 33, 51,
    203, 221, 224
Relative clauses 70
Relative pronouns 38,
    135, 138, 223, 280,
    312, 315
Repetition 43, 204, 249
Reported questions
    237
Reported speech 70,
    103, 151, 237
Representation,
    dramatic 298
Request for
    confirmation 236
Requests 149
Research 99, 294
Research, essays 120,
    121
Research, index cards
    121
Resolve 261
Respectively 249
Resumé 55
Revision, coherence
    250
Revision, editing 251
Revision, essays 121
Revision, unity 250
Rhetoric 251
Rhetorical strategies
    158
Rhyme 44
    end 252
    full 252
    internal 252
    partial 252
Rhythm 178, 253
Ridicule 256
Rise 243
Roman numerals 192
Romanticism 65, 254
Root affix 9
Rules, spelling 268
Run-on lines 112
Run-on sentences 137

Run-together sentences 72, 137

Salutation 184, 227, 255
Same 255
Sarcasm 124, 154, 158, 256
Satire 256
Scanning, poetry 179
Scansion 180
Scarcely 256
Scotch 256
Scots 256
Scottish 256
Second past 291
Second person pronouns 223
Secondary stress 011
Self pronouns 257
Semi-colons 93, 240, 257
Sentence, fragmentary 116
Sentences 19, 26, 30, 38, 53, 54, 60, 70, 71, 92, 115, 118, 130, 152, 171, 209, 220, 257, 279, 284, 298, 300, 313
  compound 71
  fragmentary 134
  fused 72, 137
  incomplete 134
  independent 71
  run-on 137
  run-together 72, 137
  topic 158, 295
Separate morphemes 145
Sequence 17
Sequence of time 285
Sexist bias 39, 123, 138, 242
Sexist language 138, 258
Shades of meaning 260

Shall 261
Shape adjectives 17
Short story, titles 239
Should 320
Sibilants 213
Significance, emotional 283
Similar 255, 261
Similar ideas 171, 206
Similarity 43
  features of 33
Similes 33, 72, 130, 262
Simple future tense 286
Simple past tense 45, 290
Simple present tense 45, 288
Simplicity 263
Single quotation marks 240
Singular 8
Singular nouns 139
Singular pronouns 22, 38, 39, 122, 138
Singular object 33
Singular verbs 39, 68, 107, 114, 188, 263
Singular, third person 46
Sites, WWW 247
Situational irony 158
Size, adjectives 17
Slang 44, 118, 127, 200, 263
Slant rhyme 252
Slogans 27
Small 264
Soliloquy 264
Somebody 265
Songs, titles 239
Sort of 265
Sounds
  consonant 27, 41, 44
  consonantal 27
  stressed 43
  vowel 42, 43
  word 134

Sources, electronic 246
South Africa 265
South Africanisms 265
Speaking, public 231
Special tenses 148
Specialist communications 161
Specific attributes 11
Specific writing 121
Speculative statements 148
Speech
  authentic 100
  colloquial 19, 38, 64
  direct 60, 100, 102, 118
  figures of 130, 144, 262
  formal 22
  indirect 103, 151
  informal 25
  parts of 11, 209
  reported 70, 103, 151, 237
Speeches
  delivery 233
  mastery of content 233
  outline 232
  preparation 232
Spelling 19, 31, 94, 101, 107, 112, 136, 159, 160, 166, 203, 208, 213, 218, 222, 265, 266, 324
Spelling rules 268
Splice, comma 71, 115, 117
Split infinitive 274
Spoken English 99, 141, 236, 249, 263
Spoken language 165, 257
Spondee 179
Standard English 225, 276, 321
Standard writing 99

Stanza 278
Statement, thesis 120, 158
Statements
  negative 37, 45
  positive 237
  speculative 148
  tentative 148
Stereotypes 66, 139, 242, 258
Strategies, rhetorical 158
Stress
  main 11
  secondary 11
  tertiary 11
Stress on words 11
Stressed sounds 43
Stressed syllables 27
Structure
  conditional 148
  deep 298
  jumbled 136
  parallel 300
  surface 298
Structures
  balanced 108
  parallel 206, 243
Style 12, 278
Style, classical 65
Subject 14, 15, 48, 63, 65, 135, 153, 163, 257 279
  plural 23
  singular 23
Subject-verb combinations 149
Subjective adjectives 17
Subjective case 63
Subjective complement 63
Subjunctive mood 183
Subordinate clauses 119, 280
Subordinating conjunctions 84, 135, 280

connectives 135
Subordination 280
Such as 281
Suffixes 10, 22, 55, 97, 134, 145, 159, 160, 201, 269, 281
Summaries 218, 282
Superfluous adjectives 54
Superfluous adverbs 54
Superlative adjectives 310
Superlative degree of comparison 18
Superlative forms 109
Supporting argument, essays 120
Surface structure 298
Surnames 213
Swear words 44, 133
Syllables 11, 27, 145, 178, 282
Symbolic connotations 283
Symbols 283
Synonyms 21, 204, 249, 283
Syntax 141, 276, 284
Synthesis, description by 97
Tag questions 37, 236
Tautology 260
Technical terms 179, 201
Technical words 161
Technical writing 7
Telegrams 7
Telexes 7
Tense
  future 261
  future perfect 287
  progressive 288
  future progressive 287, 288
  future simple 285

past 140, 142, 166, 285
past perfect progressive 291
past progressive 290
perfect 46, 176, 208
present 152
present perfect 289
present progressive 289
simple past 45, 290
simple present 45, 288
Tensed verbs 285
Tenses 119, 151
  compound 153
  future 286
  past 108
  progressive 46
  special 148
Tentative statements 148
Terminology 74
Terms
  of address 60
  ambiguous 30
  computer 74
  neutral 128
  technical 179, 201
  undefined 172
  vague 11
Terrible 292
Terrific 292
Tertiary stress 11
Tests, comprehension 74
Than 243
The 41, 293
Their 293
Theme 120, 293
Themselves 294
Theoretical possibility 47
There 293
Therefore 294
Thesaurus 284

Thesis 294
Thesis statement 120, 158
Third person pronouns 223
Third person singular 46, 138
Time 153, 195
  relations 302
  future 286
  present 288
  sequence of 285
Timetables 7
Titles 61, 184
  books 159, 295
  films 159
  music 159
  paintings 239
  poems 239
  short stories 239
  songs 239
To 297
Tone 92
Tone, melodramatic 124
Too 297
Topic sentences 120, 158, 295, 306
Toyi-toyi 297
Trademarks 62
Tragedy 69, 298
Transformational grammar 298
Transformations 299
Transitional expressions 143
Transitional phrases 135, 301
Transitional words 301
Transitions 300
Transitive verbs 55, 243, 302
Translation, idioms 147
Transparent idioms 146
Trimeter 179
Trite ideas 303
Trochee 179

Truths, general 288
Tsotsitaal 99
Two 297

Unambiguous communication 277
Uncertainty 313
Uncomparable adjectives 19
Unconscious errors 226
Uncountable nouns 32, 174
Undefined terms 172
Underlining 159, 305
Understatement 130, 306
Unified paragraph 306
Uniform metre 278
Uninflected language 188
Uninterested 104, 306
Units of measure 8
Unity 250, 306
Unity, principle of 296
Unrelated participles 208
Unrelated pronouns 115
Unspecified numbers 225
Upper case 13
Usage
  British 31
  common 41
Utility words 140

Vague expressions 265
Vague terms 11
Vague writing 30, 211
Verb-subject combinations 149
Verbs 10, 12, 14, 15, 18, 19, 28, 48, 63, 65, 108, 112, 119, 142, 149, 152, 157, 160, 163, 170, 221, 280, 282
  active 211

agreement 23
anomalous finite 35, 153
auxiliary 36, 45, 46, 135, 153, 175, 208, 235, 261, 286
base 309
finite 36, 130, 153
helping 36, 45
infinitive 142, 309
intransitive 55, 243, 303
main 130
mood 182
non-finite 130, 135, 152
ordinary 36
past participle 309
past tense form 309
plural 24, 188, 263
present participle 309
regular 35
singular 39, 68, 107, 114, 188, 263
tensed 285
transitive 55, 243, 302
Verse 27, 62, 252, 310
Verse, iambic 180
Visionary concepts 11
Viz 311
Vocabulary 31, 35, 74, 99, 140, 165, 276
Vogue words 100, 311
Voice
  active 14, 210
  passive 14, 208, 210
Vowel sounds 42, 43, 282
Vowels 33, 84, 208, 214, 311

Weak writing 211
Whether 237, 312
Which 313
While 314
Whilst 314

Who 314
Who's 314
Whom 314
Whose 314
Will 261
Word order 31, 147, 151, 318
Wordiness 14, 21, 119, 157, 198, 211, 217, 249, 315
Words
  abstract 172
  affixes 22
  anglicized 35
  archaic 294
  combination 292
  compound 73, 144
  correct arrangement of 284
  derivation 9
  elements 22
  essays 155
  feelings 127, 284
  figures of speech 130
  foreign 132, 159, 164, 165, 266, 272, 297
  four-letter 133
  hyphenation 145
  instruction 155
  loaded 128
  loan 265
  meaning 144
  misused 25, 181, 184
  negation 151
  Old English 215
  origin 160
  overworked 204, 292
  plural 216
  question 236
  sounds 134
  stress on 11
  swear 44, 133
  technical 161
  transitional 301
  utility 140
  vogue 100, 311

wrong 321
Works cited 245
Would 320
Writing
  abbreviations 122, 175
  abstract words 172
  academic 244, 249
  acknowledgement 207
  advertisements 27
  affectation 21, 264
  Afrikanerisms 154, 167
  ambiguity 48
  ambiguous 30
  anticlimax 50
  apostrophe 200, apostrophe 323
  argument 120
  attitude 129
  audience 44, 114. 249
  authentic speech 100
  awkward 42
  bathos 50
  bias 39, 123
  bibliography 51
  brackets 53
  brevity 54
  business 55
  business letters 55, 168, 255
  canon 59
  clear 67
  cliché 66, 148, 244
  clumsy 67
  clumsy expression 255
  colloquial 39
  colloquial words 68
  common errors 113, 150, 163, 238
  comparison 97
  comprehension 74
  conciseness 119
  concrete 121

conjunctions 84
connotation 127
contractions 160
contrast 158
contrasting ideas 143
convoluted expressions 168
creative 129
curriculum vitae 89
dash 92
denotation 127
description 97
dialogue 100, 104
direct speech 100
dramatic overstatement 144
dull 149
editing 251
electronic sources 247
ellipsis 109
emotive 128
emphasis 028, 038, 123, 159, 177
epic 112
essays 120
euphemism 122, 316
exaggeration 123, 144
example 97
excerpts 124
feelings 129
figurative devices 306
figurative language 129
figures of speech 130, 144, 177
final draft 219
first draft 120
footnotes 131, 207
foreign words 133, 159, 164, 266
formal 9, 22, 35, 90, 92, 122, 134, 148, 187, 231
formulation 74
function 97
generalizations 117, 139, 172